Joyce XMAS 1993

HAMLYN ALL COLOUR GUIDE TO DOGS

Special photography by Ray Moller

Designed by Town Group Consultancy Ltd

First published in Great Britain in 1993 by Hamlyn,
an imprint of Reed Consumer Books Limited,
part of Reed International Books Limited,
Michelin House,
81 Fulham Road,
London SW3 6RB
and Auckland, Melbourne, Singapore and Toronto

ISBN 0 600 58012 1

A catalogue record for this book is available
from the British Library.

Produced by Mandarin Offset

Printed in Hong Kong

HAMLYN ALL COLOUR GUIDE TO DOGS

Susan Egerton-Jones & Caroline Taggart

HAMLYN

Contents

Working Dogs

Toys

Introduction

Dogs have been 'man's best friend' for many thousands of years and over the years we have used them to help us hunt for food, to guard our homes and our livestock, to pull vehicles and to keep us company.

Dogs are descended from wolves, which were once much more common and more widely distributed around the world than they are now. Wolves themselves came in various shapes and sizes, so even the earliest dogs differed in type from one part of the world to the next. When humans began to domesticate wolves, each society had differing needs. Those who wanted a guard for their herds looked for alertness and reliability, while northern peoples who wanted animals to pull their sleds were interested in strength and stamina. So over many centuries, the early wolf-like dog evolved into the hundreds of breeds, and thousands of non-breeds, we know today.

Some breeds are generally more even-tempered than others. If a breed is usually 'good' with children – like the Labrador shown here – or rather unreliable, this is indicated in the entries in the book. But all dogs are individuals and their temperament should not be taken for granted. The key factor is proper training of both dogs and children.

The Breed Groups

All the major canine organizations of the world divide pedigree dogs into groups or categories of breeds for the purposes of registration and showing. The Kennel Club of Great Britain (KC) has six:

1. *Gundogs* were bred not to hunt but to accompany the hunter and flush out or retrieve game. Many of the world's most popular breeds, including the spaniels, retrievers and setters, belong to this group.

2. *Hounds* were the true hunters. This group divides roughly into two categories: those bred for their speed and keen sight, and those used in packs to sniff out a quarry. The sighthounds include the Borzoi and the Greyhound; the scenthounds include Beagles and Basset Hounds.

3. *Terriers* are usually small dogs bred to go down foxholes and badger setts. These are tough, alert dogs with minds of their own. The West Highland White and the Cairn look like typical terriers.

4. *Utility Dogs* comprise the catch-all group which includes such diverse breeds as the Lhasa Apso, the Dalmatian, the Poodle and the Chow Chow.

5. *Working Dogs* were the shepherds and guardians of the flocks and herds. The group encompasses breeds as disparate as the Welsh Corgi and the Pyrenean Mountain Dog.

6. *Toy Dogs* are the small creatures bred as pets and companions. Despite the designation 'toy', the dogs in this group are often tough and strong-willed. The Pekingese, the Yorkshire Terrier and the Cavalier King Charles Spaniel are among the most popular Toy breeds.

At the time of writing, a working committee of the Kennel Club of Great Britain is considering these groupings and the next eighteen months may well see changes in the classification.

The American Kennel Club (AKC), Canadian Kennel Club (CKC) and Australian National Kennel Council (ANKC) all have seven groups. The classification of a breed as a Gundog (known as a Sporting Dog in North America), Hound, Terrier or Toy is usually the same throughout the world. The breeds classed as Working and Utility in Britain are divided into Herding, Working and Non-sporting Dogs in North America, while the ANKC has Working, Utility and Non-sporting classes. The AKC and CKC groupings and standards are almost identical – in the entries in this book, separate information is given for Canada only when it differs from that of the United States.

Choosing a Dog

A respectable breeder will encourage you to visit before you commit yourself to buying a puppy, and will be able to provide proof of soundness of stock. This is particularly important with the popular 'family' breeds, where overbreeding has sometimes led to faults in temperament and soundness. Overbreeding can also exaggerate any health problems to which a breed may be prone. This Bulldog has a strong, healthy head, but a more 'squashed in' nose could lead to breathing difficulties.

Before you acquire any kind of dog, you should ask yourself what you want from it – and what you don't want. If you have small children you should be very careful to select a dog with an even temper. If you live in a lonely country house, you may want a breed with strong territorial instincts that will warn you of intruders; on the other hand, if you have lots of visitors, this could be a nuisance. The entries in this book are designed to help you choose a breed that suits your circumstances.

You should consider whether you want a puppy or an adult dog. An adult dog may have bad habits that will be difficult to break – it is much easier to train a puppy to fit in with your lifestyle. On the other hand, training a puppy requires time and patience, and any adult dog you acquire will almost certainly have had some training.

Should you have a dog or a bitch? With smaller dogs there is rarely any great difference in temperament between the sexes, but some larger dogs are more aggressive than bitches of the same breed. They may also be more protective of their territory and have a tendency to wander. If you buy a bitch, you have to be prepared to deal with her, and with the males living nearby when she is in season.

Buying a Pedigree Dog

Always go to a respectable breeder. Kennel clubs and breed societies keep lists. A successful breeder may not be able to let you have a dog straight away, as the puppies may be booked well in advance. Be patient – it is worth waiting for the right pet. You should be able to reserve a puppy of a specified sex from an unborn litter, then choose the individual you want when the puppy is about six weeks old. You normally collect the puppy when it is about eight weeks old (when it has been weaned). The breeder should supply you with vaccination certificates, records of the dog's pedigree and registration and advice on feeding.

Buying a Mongrel or Crossbreed

You may not want a pedigree dog. A friend may own a bitch that has unexpectedly had puppies, or you may feel that you want to give a home to one of the many abandoned dogs in dogs' homes or rescue centres.

If you are buying privately, you may know nothing about the father of the puppies, but you can inspect the conditions in which the bitch and the puppies are being kept; if these are satisfactory and the bitch and puppies are healthy, you should acquire a sound pet.

With a 'rescue' dog, you will have less certainty. It will have been well looked after and had all the necessary injections since it came into care, but that may be all you know. Many such dogs have been ill treated as well as abandoned, and this may mean they have behavioural problems that will take a long time, patience and a lot of affection to put right.

Never acquire a dog for purely emotional reasons. Remember that you are taking on a commitment that could last 15 years or even longer.

Your Dog's Health

It is sensible to speak to a vet before you acquire a dog. Personal recommendation is best. Talk to your friends and neighbours who have dogs. Take your puppy for a full check-up within 48 hours of bringing it home and make sure you know the practice's emergency phone number. You should ask your vet for advice on such matters as insurance, diet, vaccinations, worming and any regular health checks that may be necessary.

Caring for Your Dog

Before you take your new dog, whether puppy or adult home, you should have made basic preparations to receive it. Decide where it is to sleep and always keep its bed in the same place. Remember that dogs like human company and should not be made to feel cut off from the family when they go to bed.

Choose a place for your dog's food and water bowls. All dogs need a constant supply of fresh water and regular mealtimes. When you first bring a puppy home, follow the feeding pattern it is used to for the first few weeks; you may upset its digestive system if you give it unfamiliar food. If its mealtimes are inconvenient for you, change them gradually.

The amount a dog eats varies enormously. A tiny toy breed may only need 100 g (3-4 oz) of canned food a day, while an active retriever may eat five or six times that amount and an Irish Wolfhound – shown here – even more. Whether you feed an adult dog canned food, a complete diet or meat and biscuits is largely up to you. There are many products on the market and you should experiment to establish the diet that best suits your dog. Choosing good quality food is particularly important with puppies to ensure proper bone and muscle development. Dogs mature at different rates and many large breeds do not reach full maturity until they are two years old.

Grooming should become part of your dog's routine from the start. Handle the dog gently but firmly and it will soon become accustomed to regular brushing and combing. Long-haired dogs like this Rough Collie should be groomed every day.

Puppies, like children, need frequent small meals – four, evenly spaced throughout the day, at the age of two to three months. Meals should gradually increase in size and decrease in number until the dog is one to two years old; most mature dogs have only one main meal a day.

Other elements of basic daily care, notably exercise and grooming, are dealt with in the individual entries in this book and in 'care tips' that apply both to individual breeds as well as other breeds and types of dog.

Basic Training

This is essential and requires a lot of patience: a puppy is bound to make mistakes, particularly when it comes to house training. Put newspaper by the door and encourage your dog to use it. If you have enough warning, you can quickly take the newspaper outside, so that the dog becomes used to the idea of going outside to relieve itself.

Teach your dog its name by using it every time you speak to it. Simple commands such as 'come', 'sit' and 'stay' should be practised whenever the opportunity arises. Most dogs are naturally eager to please, and fulsome praise when your dog gets something right will help to get the action repeated. Scold only if you catch it making a mistake. If you find out later and are angry, the dog will not understand.

Socialization is important in a puppy's life: dogs which are not used to human companionship from an early age may become over-possessive of their owners and hostile to strangers. Dogs which are not used to other dogs may be aggressive. Make sure children treat dogs with respect. And keep an eye on other pets when you bring a new dog home. Two or more animals living in the same household will soon sort out a pecking order, but there may be friction at first.

A Final Checklist

Before you decide to acquire a dog, ask yourself the following questions:

• Can you give a dog a good home? • Can you afford to feed it correctly, pay vet's fees and insurance and arrange proper care if you go away? • Are you prepared to train it, exercise it, groom it and give it plenty of affection? • Do you know how much time this will take every day? • Will your home accommodate a dog and allow it some space of its own?

If you can honestly answer yes to all these questions, go ahead and get a dog. There are few joys greater than the companionship of an affectionate, well-trained dog. I hope this book will encourage you to choose your pet wisely, treat it well and enjoy it to the full.

SOLOMON

Dachshund

The Dachshund's low-slung body makes it ideal for the purpose for which it was bred – worming its way into badger setts. The courage that enabled it to take on the much larger badger is still a feature of its nature.

It is possible that the Dachshund was known in ancient times, but the modern breed was developed in Germany in the 18th century. Until the late 19th century, only the smooth-haired Dachshund was recognized. Nowadays there are six varieties – smooth-haired, long-haired and wire-haired, with miniature versions of each – but they are considered to be one breed, differing only in size and type of coat.

The Dachshund's classification as a hound is the result of a mistranslation (the German *hund* means dog, not specifically hound), and in its working life it is really more of a terrier. Dachshund means 'badger dog' and its original job was to hunt badgers. It has great courage, a keen sense of smell and an enthusiasm for burrowing that could make it an undesirable pet for committed gardeners.

Its long body means that the Dachshund is prone to back problems; in old age it may also run to fat. These small dogs do not need much exercise, but they do need some. Like all long-haired dogs, the long-haired Dachshund needs frequent grooming, and the wire-haired benefits from stripping.

Properly trained, Dachshunds make affectionate and good-natured companions. They are fiercely loyal to their owners and will defend them against opponents much bigger than themselves.

COAT

Smooth-haired short, dense and shiny; wire-haired short and coarse; long-haired silky with a slight wave and feathering on legs. The most common colours are red, black or black and tan.

HEIGHT

About 12-22 cm (5-9 in).

HEAD

Held confidently high. Long and narrow. Broad, rounded ears are set high on the head and hang close to it. Medium-sized, almond-shaped eyes are usually dark.

NECK

Long, strong, slightly arched.

BODY

Long and muscular, with a straight back. Not so close to the ground as to restrict movement.

LEGS

Short and strong, the back legs in particular should be straight and wide set. Rather large, round feet.

TAIL

Set high on body, slightly curved, tapering and carried level with the back.

GROUP

Hound.

Beagle

The Beagle has an attractive appearance and an appealing expression, belying its determined character. Its nature, however, is sociable and it is affectionate with children and other dogs.

COAT

Comes in all the hound colours both tri- and bicolour and is short and dense.

HEIGHT

33-41 cm (13-16 in). In North America 38 cm (15 in) is the maximum.

HEAD

Fairly long with flattish, domed skull, well-defined stop and squarish muzzle, finer in the bitch. Expressive, fairly large, dark brown to hazel eyes. Long, round tipped ears are set low.

NECK

Strong and slightly arched.

BODY

Well-balanced overall with well let-down chest and well-sprung ribs. The back is strong and straight with powerful loins.

LEGS

Muscular, straight and strong with round, strongly padded feet and arched toes.

TAIL

Thick at the base and tapering, set high.

GROUP

Hound.

Individual Beagles kept as pets are a comparatively recent development in this small hound's history which goes back more than 400 years in Europe. Used for pack and sometimes pair hunting and even retrieving, this scent hound is followed on foot or on horseback mainly on the trail of hares but also in pursuit of other small game such as jackal and wild pig. It is the smallest of the English hounds and in the past was bred even smaller than it is now.

Cheerful and friendly as a companion dog, the Beagle requires firm training and control as once on a scent it can stubbornly refuse to obey commands. It loves its food and will quickly run to fat unless it is very well exercised and its diet controlled. It is easy to keep, needing only light grooming, though its ears should be regularly checked and kept clean.

CARE TIP

Dog collars are available in a variety of sizes and materials. The only essentials are that they should be tough, and fit securely enough to avoid being slipped but be loose enough not to restrict the neck. Identification tags should be attached to the dog collar so that owners may be traced quickly if a dog is found wandering – a common trait that is particularly strong in scent dogs.

Petit Basset Griffon Vendeen

◄ *The merry, rough appearance of the Petit Basset Griffon Vendeen clearly represents its clownish approach to life. It has a fine reputation with children and makes a good companion, but needs firm training to control its hunting instincts.*

Vendeen Griffons have been bred in Western France as powerful hunters, but of the four varieties it is the Petit Basset, or PBGV, as it is often called, that has surfaced from its working background and been increasingly valued as an adaptable family pet.

Rough-coated, short-legged and with a friendly nature, the PBGV was officially recognized in Britain in 1950. It is a lively and intelligent little dog that does best when living where open country is easily accessible for good, long runs. Its rough coat is easy to maintain with a hard brush and comb.

The PBGV is known by a number of other names: the Small Griffon Vendeen, Small Vendeen Basset and Basset Griffon Vendeen (Petit).

CARE TIP

Rough-coated dogs are usually easy to keep clean. When conditions are wet and muddy, a stiff brush and a comb are best applied after the coat has dried off.

COAT

Longish, harsh rough top coat with a thick undercoat. In combinations of lemon, orange, grizzle or tricolour on white.

HEIGHT

About 33-38 cm (13-15 in).

HEAD

Of reasonable width and medium length with a definite stop and occipital bone and well-developed jaws. Dark brown, friendly eyes. Quite narrow, oval ears set low.

NECK

Quite long and strong.

BODY

Deep chest with a prominent sternum; longish, level back with slight arching over strong loins.

LEGS

Strong and sturdy; slight crook acceptable on forelegs; hard, tight-padded feet.

TAIL

Carried like a sabre, set high with a gradual taper from a strong base.

GROUP

Hound.

Basset Hound

The wrinkly face, lugubrious eyes, long ears and a kindly nature have made the Basset Hound a much loved family dog. ▶

COAT

Smooth and short in any recognized hound colour.

HEIGHT

33-38 cm (13-15 in). In North America, 35 cm (14 in) is the maximum.

HEAD

Broad and long. Skin hangs loosely over the skull, giving furrowed brows and overhanging upper lip. Lozenge-shaped eyes are normally dark. Ears are low-set, long, drooping and velvety.

NECK

Longish, powerful and arched, with definite dewlap.

BODY

Long and deep, with broad, practically level back.

LEGS

Short and sturdy, again with loose skin giving a wrinkled appearance. Slightly inward-curving front legs should not touch or inhibit movement. Very large feet for the size of the dog.

TAIL

Long, strong and tapering, with some coarse hair underneath.

GROUP

Hound.

The Basset Hound was French in origin, arising from dwarfism in other hounds, and then bred on to become a' scent hunter in dense undergrowth. The breed was refined and developed in Britain using Bloodhound stock. Basset packs are still found in Britain and are prized not only for their impressive scenting ability but also for their stamina and relentless perseverance. The Basset's affectionate nature has also ensured its position as a family pet.

This is a strong dog and requires plenty of steady exercise to retain musculature and suppleness. It is inclined to be independent and requires consistent and continuous discipline to control a tendency to wander. A Basset is happiest with its nose to the ground, but this can increase the risk of infection and careful watch should be kept for any such telltale signs. The long ears should also be checked and cleaned regularly.

Potential buyers of Bassets should look for puppies with the straightest limbs from stock that has no history of back problems. A healthy Basset is affectionate, free of vice and good with children.

CARE TIP

Dogs with very long ears eat more cleanly out of feeding bowls with high sides. Whatever shape of bowl is used for the dog, it is important to ensure that it doesn't tip up too easily.

Basenji

◄ *The appeal of the Basenji lies in its fun-loving disposition. Its expression is alert, and it is always ready for mischief.*

The Basenji, or Congo Dog, is best known for not having a bark, but it has other characteristics that make it an ideal pet, notably an almost cat-like attention to personal hygiene, and an affectionate disposition. It is particularly good with children. A Basenji should not be kept in an outside kennel; it is essentially a house dog that will take over the sofa if you let it. It is active and requires plenty of exercise, and its short coat needs minimum grooming.

The Basenji may have originated in Ancient Egypt, where carvings of similar looking dogs have been found in the tombs of pharaohs. It was brought to Britain in the 19th century from Central Africa, where it was used for tracking and as a guard dog. Breeding it outside Africa was found to be difficult, as it proved very vulnerable to distemper. As a result, the 'Bush Dog' did not appear at Crufts until 1937 and only became established in the United States in the early 1940s.

Although it does not bark in the conventional sense, it growls and whines like other dogs and also emits a cheerful yodelling sound. The wrinkles on its forehead give it an enquiring look that fits in well with its inquisitive nature.

COAT

Short, fine, silky hair over loosely fitting skin. It can be red, black or black and tan, but all colours have a white chest, feet and tail tip.

HEIGHT

Dog: 43 cm (17 in); bitch: 40 cm (16 in).

HEAD

Flat and of medium width, finely chiselled, tapering towards the nose. Slight stop. The characteristic wrinkles should not be exaggerated. Dark, almond-shaped eyes. Ears set well forward, small and erect.

NECK

Long, strong but not thick. A graceful curve should allow the head to be carried high.

BODY

Lightly built with deep rib cage and short, level back.

LEGS

Long for the size of the dog, straight with sturdy thighs. Small feet.

TAIL

High set, curling tightly over spine and lying against the thigh, sometimes with a second curl.

GROUP

Hound.

Whippet

The Whippet may look dainty, but it is a fast, strong, sporting dog and with all the qualities of an ideal family pet.

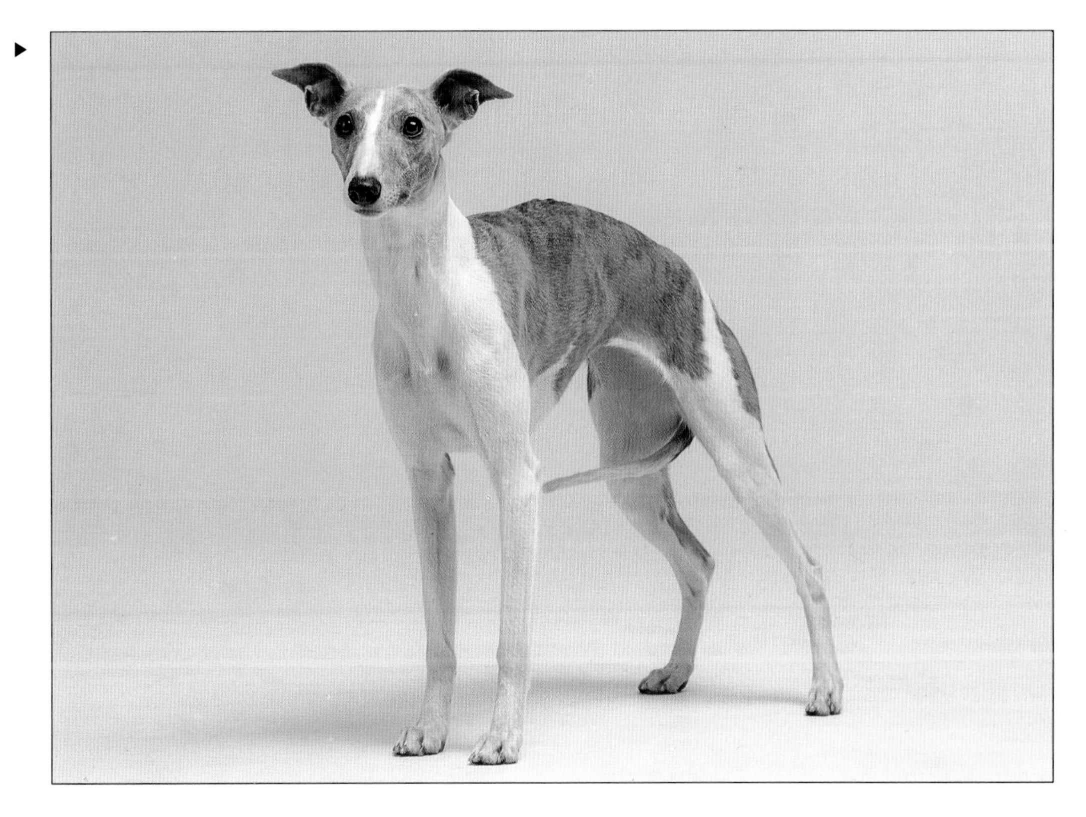

Developed in the North of England by sports-minded working folk who wanted an easier and less expensive coursing dog than the Greyhound, the Whippet's ancestors are rather obscure; however, it undoubtedly owes its strong, graceful lines to Middle Eastern sight hounds.

It was recognized as a breed at the end of the 19th century and since then has gained wide popularity both as a sporting dog and as a gentle, affectionate, obedient pet. The Whippet is a sturdy, healthy dog, combining elegance with a surprisingly powerful frame. Its only weakness is that it does not like to get wet.

It has an ideal temperament for the show ring and makes few demands on its owners other than a warm blanket to curl up in indoors, light grooming and enough regular exercise to keep fit for whatever duties it may be asked to perform.

COAT

Fine, short and close, in all shades and mixtures.

HEIGHT

Dog: about 47-56 cm (18-22 in); bitch: about 44-53 cm (17-21 in).

HEAD

Flat topped, long and lean; quite wide between the eyes, tapering to a fine muzzle. Dark, lively, oval eyes. Small rose-shaped ears.

NECK

Arched, muscular and long.

BODY

Deep-chested with well-sprung ribs; muscular back arched over the loins.

LEGS

Length in proportion to body, strong and muscular with strongly padded feet and well-spaced toes.

TAIL

Tapering, with a curve.

GROUP

Hound.

CARE TIP

A dimpled handmitten or chamois leather is the best grooming equipment for fine-haired dogs. Unlike many smaller breeds, the Whippet takes about two years to develop to full maturity and its diet and exercise regimes should be planned accordingly.

Saluki

◀ *One of the most beautiful of the hounds, the graceful, elegant lines of this hunting dog belie its strong constitution and intelligence.*

One of the very earliest pure breeds of dog, the Saluki today probably looks much as it did 9000 years ago. Its origins lie in the Middle East and for centuries it was the prized sight hound of Bedouin tribes, pampered and treated with affection by people who considered their sheepdogs 'unclean'. Even today a few of these dogs are kept in the modern Arab world to hunt with falcons and to course the increasingly rare gazelle, fox and hare. In the West, the Saluki was officially recognized as a breed in the early 20th century and the dog is better known as a show dog and pet.

Though friendly and loyal, the Saluki has a rather sensitive nature and demands gentle but consistent training and handling to keep its natural hunting instincts under control. It adapts well to most environments and is easy to keep as long as it can exercise safely and freely and has plenty of companionship.

As well as possessing a striking-looking coat, the Saluki has strange, distinctive feet. The toes are slightly webbed and the two inner toes are noticeably longer than the outer on all four feet. This must help them retain their footing on the rugged terrain of their native land.

COAT

Long and of a smooth, silky texture with light feathering on the body and with more obvious feathering on the ears and tail. The smooth-haired variety has no feathering. White, cream, fawn, golden, red, grey/grizzle, black and tan, tricolour and fringed variations of these colours.

HEIGHT

Dogs between 58-71 cm (23-28 in); bitches smaller.

HEAD

Long and narrow, with a comparatively wide skull. The eyes are expressive, oval and dark to hazel in colour. The mobile ears are fairly long and hairy.

NECK

Long, supple and muscular.

BODY

Long, deep brisket, broad back slightly arched.

LEGS

Long and well-muscled. The feet are strong and supple, with slightly webbed toes.

TAIL

Set low and carried naturally in a curve.

GROUP

Hound.

Bloodhound

The Bloodhound's famous sorrowful expression is not inappropriate for this sensitive dog. Let it loose in the country, however, where it can investigate an exciting variety of scents and it will be very happy indeed. ▶

COAT

Smooth and short haired. Black and tan, liver and tan or red.

HEIGHT

Dog: 63-69 cm (25-27 in); bitch: 58-63 cm (23-25 in).

HEAD

Long and narrow, covered with loose skin. Pronounced occipital peak. Long, drooping upper lip and jowls. The ears are long, soft and drooping. Medium-sized, oval eyes, either dark brown or hazel. The eyes should not be deeply sunken or the eyebrows very prominent, but the folds of loose skin may give this appearance.

NECK

Long, covered in loose skin.

BODY

Solid, with deep brisket, muscular shoulders, broad back and slightly arched loins.

LEGS

Very straight forelegs; strong, muscular hind legs.

TAIL

Long, thick at base but tapering to a point.

GROUP

Hound.

The St Hubert Hound was bred at St Hubert's Abbey in the Ardennes region of Belgium as early as the 8th century. Popular with the kings of France for hundreds of years, it crossed the Channel with William the Conqueror and was established as the favoured English royal hound. The name 'Bloodhound' probably refers to the purity of the dog's lineage rather than to its hunting instincts, although its tracking 'nose' is second to none.

The Bloodhound makes an affectionate pet and is good with children, but prospective owners should be aware of what they are taking on. This is a large dog which requires plenty of space – it really should not be kept in a town. It needs lots of exercise and is likely to come back from a run covered in mud having investigated every ditch in sight. Its coat is easy to clean, however, so the dirt should not be too much of a problem to get rid of.

The Bloodhound is perhaps surprisingly sensitive, so it should not be smacked or subjected to any form of physical punishment during training.

The breed is susceptible to a serious stomach complaint known as torsion, which occurs when gases build up inside the stomach, causing bloating. This is a cause for concern and can be fatal if it does not receive immediate veterinary attention. Consult your vet so that you know what symptoms to look out for.

The American Coonhounds are related to the Bloodhound, having been bred from European hounds to hunt raccoon.

Rhodesian Ridgeback

The Rhodesian Ridgeback was in fact first developed in South Africa. The ridge of reverse-facing hair running from two identical crowns at the shoulder and tapering to the haunches is a distinguishing feature.

Farmers in Southern Africa developed the Ridgeback to hunt in packs, their quarry being lions and other large game. Its alternative name of African Lion Hound harks back to this original purpose. The distinctive ridge of an ancient Hottentot dog is a guide to at least one of its ancestors, the Great Dane is believed to be another and other imported European farm breeds make up the rest. This genealogy is slightly more complicated than it would seem, however. The only other 'ridgeback' breed, the Phu Quoc Dog, originated in an island off Thailand. It may have been brought to Africa centuries ago by Phoenician traders, and interbreeding with native African dogs may have ensured the survival of the ridgeback, although the Asian breed is probably now extinct.

The usefulness of the Ridgeback as a quiet and effective guard dog was quickly recognized and its affectionate, gentle nature has ensured its popularity as a family pet. Naturally rather lazy, it is easy to keep, requiring only human companionship and light grooming, but regular exercise and space to run freely are important if it is to keep fit.

COAT

Thick, short and glossy, wheaten to red in colour.

HEIGHT

Dog: about 63-68 cm (25-27 in); bitch: about 61-66 cm (24-26 in).

HEAD

Fairly long with flat, broad skull, reasonable stop and long, powerful jaws. The intelligent round eyes tone with the coat. Rather wide, tapering ears hang close to the head.

NECK

Quite long and strong.

BODY

Deep, capacious chest with moderately well-sprung ribs, powerful back and muscular, slightly arched loins.

LEGS

Proportionately strong and muscular with feet protected by hair between well-arched toes and tough pads.

TAIL

Strong, slightly tapering in a gentle curve.

GROUP

Hound.

Afghan Hound

The Afghan Hound is the major star of any dog show. Its height and flowing coat, its aristocratic face and impressive jaws are enhanced by its evident love of life. ▶

COAT

Acceptable in all colours, the hair of the coat is luxuriantly long and fine, short on the face with a distinctive 'top knot', and short along the back.

HEIGHT

Dog: 66-74 cm (26-29 in); bitch 60-69 cm (23-27 in). Smaller in North America.

HEAD

Widish skull with prominent occiput, slight stop and long, impressive jaws. Rather an aloof expression in its usually dark, slanted eyes. Long, hairy ears are set low.

NECK

Long and strong.

BODY

Deep chest; well-sprung ribs; moderately long, level back; broad, rather short loins.

LEGS

Long, straight and strong with large, strong forefeet, slightly smaller hind feet; all four feet well-covered with long hair.

TAIL

Set low and sparsely feathered, curled in a ring at the end.

GROUP

Hound.

The origins of the Afghan almost certainly lie in the Middle East thousands of years ago; from there the greyhound-type dog travelled, probably via Persia, to the harsh landscape and the homes of the tribal chiefs and nobles of Afghanistan. The development of the Afghan's superb coat protected it against the harsh climate of the region, and its abilities as a hunter of large game and as a herd guard ensured its value and survival through the centuries. It was so highly esteemed in its native land that selling it to outsiders was prohibited until the beginning of the 20th century. First imported into the UK in 1907, it made a spectacular début at the Crystal Palace. The Afghan breed was officially recognized in Britain in 1926, and in North America a few years later.

Loyal, affectionate to its family and very glamorous, the Afghan makes an excellent pet. Independent and very energetic, with strong hunting instincts, this dog requires sensitive, but firm, continuous discipline and plenty of hard exercise. Its coat should be groomed regularly with a long-bristled brush; ears and feet should be checked very often as matted hair can cause considerable discomfort and ear infections are always a possibility with long-eared dogs.

Borzoi

◀ *The profile of the Borzoi is one of its most distinctive features, being long, narrow and almost straight. Running at full stretch, the dog is a picture of power and speed.*

The Borzoi, or Russian Wolfhound, was developed in Imperial Russia as a fast and powerful hunter of wolves. Either Asian or Middle Eastern in origin, both its appearance and its hunting ability were highly regarded by the nobility from the 15th century, and its stamina and intelligence were enhanced by introducing sheepdog and other hound strains. By the mid 19th century Borzois as we know them today were to be seen in many of the great houses of Europe.

The quiet, rather aloof nature of this large dog has earned it a place as a loyal family pet, though it prefers the companionship of adults to that of children and it is not a breed which indulges in boisterous games. It needs to be sensitively disciplined and extensively exercised when mature. It retains its hunting instincts and so should not be allowed to run loose if there is livestock around. It must also be regularly groomed to maintain the condition of its well-feathered coat.

The Borzoi has a good appetite and demands nourishing food. This should be given two or three times a day to avoid the stomach torsion that may occur after bolting a large meal. The puppies take at least two years to reach maturity and require a carefully controlled diet and limited exercise to ensure strong bones.

COAT

The silky hair is short on the face, ears and front of the legs, long over the body with profuse feathering and there is a curly frill round the neck. Most colour combinations, usually with white predominating.

HEIGHT

Dog: about 70-82 cm (27-32 in); bitch: about 65-77 cm (25-30 in).

HEAD

Long and lean with slightly domed skull and long, powerful jaws. Dark, almond-shaped eyes. The ears are quite small, pointed and set high.

NECK

Fairly long, muscular and slightly arched.

BODY

Very deep brisket with narrow, oval ribs, and tucked up abdomen. The back rises from the powerful loin in a graceful curve.

LEGS

Long, and strong, with arched oval feet.

TAIL

Well-feathered, set and carried low in a gentle curve.

GROUP

Hound.

Greyhound

The fine coat of the Greyhound shows off its athletic structure and well-developed musculature. It is a clean dog and its fine coat requires only light brushing or finishing with a mitten or chamois leather. ▶

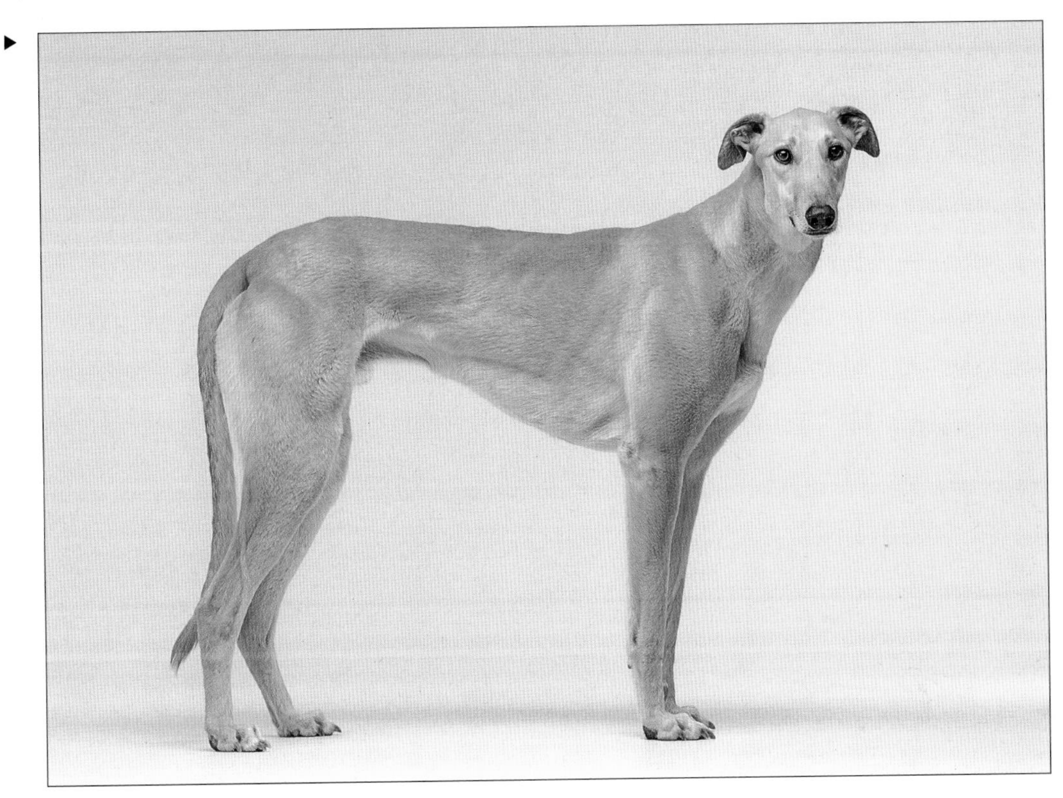

COAT

In all colours and parti-colours, short, tight and silky.

HEIGHT

Dog: about 71-76 cm (28-30 in); bitch: about 69-71 cm (27-28 in).

HEAD

Long, flat, moderately wide skull with a slight stop and long, powerful jaws. Dark, intelligent, obliquely set eyes. Small, rose-shaped ears.

NECK

Long, strong and arched.

BODY

Deep-chested with well-sprung ribs and well cut-up belly; the back is long and strong with arched, powerful loins.

LEGS

Long and strong, with distinctive, wide muscular thighs and long, strongly padded feet.

TAIL

Set rather low, tapering and curved.

GROUP

Hound.

The history of the Greyhound is filled with outstanding sporting achievements. Its breed has remained pure for thousands of years and pictorial records of the dog exist from Ancient Egyptian times, from between 5000 to 4000 BC.

The Greyhound today is bred for three activities: racing (it will reach speeds of well over 65 km (40 miles) per hour chasing the electric hare on the racetrack); coursing live hares across open country; and showing. The size and build of the dog will vary depending on the role it has been bred for.

The breed has a well-developed instinct for hunting and killing prey. So while a greyhound will make a gentle, affectionate, loyal and intelligent pet and be neat and clean in the house, other small household pets could be at risk as soon as they decide to make a run for it. Naturally lazy, it requires quite a specific diet, training and exercise to develop its full potential in the field for which it was bred.

CARE TIP

The slip leash is designed for fast control, quick to release when coursing, easy to fit, and light and safe for training and showing. Greyhounds have long, delicate necks and require special collars.

Irish Wolfhound

The Irish Wolfhound is truly majestic in appearance and its character is one of the finest – it is only roused if excessively provoked. It is happiest as a house dog, though its size means the home has to be fairly spacious.

This legendary hound of Ireland is a gentle giant of a dog. Its early ancestors can only be guessed at, but its history is over 2000 years old, pre-dating the Roman occupation. It was used to hunt and kill wolves and as a guard, and was highly valued, often being presented as a gift to favoured foreign potentates.

By the 19th century, however, the breed had virtually disappeared, together with the gradual extinction of the wolf in Ireland, and it was only through the efforts of a Captain George Graham that the Wolfhound was re-established and first registered in the late 19th century.

Stories about the loyalty and intelligence of the Wolfhound abound, and despite its size it remains a popular family pet with an excellent reputation with children.

Puppies need care and special feeding through to maturity at three years to ensure that growing bones and muscles are not stressed. Although hard exercise is not essential for the adult dog, it must have regular walks and plenty of space.

CARE TIP

Large dogs are more comfortably controlled with short leads. Strong, fast animals need to be trained to walk quietly on the leash and to respond to commands. The type, size and length of leash are determined by the type and size of dog and the amount of exercise or range of activity it is being asked to pursue.

COAT

Rough and harsh with shaggy eyebrows and a shaggy coat under the chin. Dark to light grey, black, white, brindle, fawn, sandy or red are all permitted colours.

HEIGHT

(Minimum) dog: 79 cm (31 in); bitch 71 cm (28 in). Both sexes are 2.5 cm (1 in) or more larger in North America.

HEAD

Long, with a slightly raised forehead, not too broad a skull and a long, moderately pointed muzzle. Full, dark, oval eyes. Rather small ears, usually carried folded back.

NECK

Arched, long and strong.

BODY

Deep, wide chest with well drawn-up belly, longish back and arched loins.

LEGS

Muscular and strong. Largish, round feet with arched toes.

TAIL

Quite thick and slightly curved.

GROUP

Hound.

American Cocker Spaniel

The hunting skills and athleticism of the American Cocker Spaniel should never be overlooked when admiring the charm and appeal of this deservedly popular family pet.

COAT

Long, flat or slightly wavy, finer on head with luxuriant feathering on ears, chest, abdomen and legs. Accepted show colours range from lightest buff to black, parti-colours and tricolour.

HEIGHT

34-39 cm (13½-15½ in). In North America 38 cm (15 in) is the maximum.

HEAD

Well-developed and rounded with broad, square jaws. Intelligent, soft, round, dark eyes. Very long, heavy ears set at eye level.

NECK

Long, muscular and slightly arched.

BODY

Compact, strong, slightly sloping back to widish, muscular hindquarters.

LEGS

Well-boned and muscular. The compact, round feet have tough pads with hair between them.

TAIL

Carried on line with back and frequently wagged.

GROUP

Gundog (KC, ANKC). Sporting (AKC).

The American Cocker shares common ancestors with the English Cocker, having been selectively bred from stock imported into the United States in the late 19th century. Smaller than the English Cocker, with proportionately longer legs, the American was quickly recognized as a valuable hunter. It achieved its own status in the 1940s.

Today, it is more popular as a family pet and show dog than as a working dog, but it still retains its hunting prowess and sporting instincts. Companionable, biddable, adaptable and lively, this attractive character needs plenty of exercise and regular grooming and occasional trimming to maintain its superb coat. Check the ears and feet regularly to avoid build up of infection and balling.

Like many popular dogs, the American Cocker has sometimes suffered from over-breeding. It is particularly important to buy from a reputable breeder and to select a puppy which shows no signs of nervousness or snappishness.

Cocker Spaniel

◀ *The silky coat of the English Cocker Spaniel requires very regular grooming and occasional trimming. Particular attention should be paid to keeping the ears and feet clean of seeds, bits of undergrowth and mud.*

Many European spaniels were used for hunting purposes by the time of the 14th century and are probably descended from a type originating from Spain – the old French name *Espaignol* certainly suggests this. Spaniels have always been valued for their scenting powers and for their flushing and retrieving abilities. The Cocker Spaniel was developed in England to 'cock' or point and flush woodcock, and was fully established by the late 19th century.

It remains an excellent all-purpose gundog, but its happy, gentle nature, intelligence and size, as well as its attractive appearance, have earned it its high rating as a family pet. Its ebullient nature does mean that firm, early training is required. It has a good reputation with children, though care should be taken when it is first introduced into the family. It will quickly run to fat if not given plenty of exercise. In some lines of solid colours there have been a few problems with temperament, so puppies should be selected with care.

CARE TIP

A pre-formed, washable dog bed, with a washable liner, is both easily portable and hygienic. Available in many sizes, they are particularly valuable for dogs with long coats that are frequently wet and mud spattered after exercise.

COAT

Flat and silky with ample feathering. All mixtures as well as solid colours with a little white allowed on the chest.

HEIGHT

Dog: about 39-40 cm (15½-16 in); bitch: about 38-39 cm (15-15½ in).

HEAD

Fairly long and lean with well-developed skull, moderately prominent occipital bone, well-defined stop, square muzzle and strong jaws. Soft, dark brown eyes. Long, large ears hang from eye level.

NECK

Muscular, fairly long, and well-set in sloping shoulders.

BODY

Short-backed, compact, well coupled with a broad, deep chest and short muscular loins.

LEGS

Muscular, straight with well let-down, long hocks and firm, well-padded, cat-like feet.

TAIL

Feathered, very waggy and carried in line. Has traditionally been docked.

GROUP

Gundog (KC, ANKC). Sporting (AKC).

English Springer Spaniel

The Springer's distinctive coat is not difficult to maintain in good condition with brushing, but as with all the spaniels, its ears and feet should be regularly and carefully checked. ▶

COAT

Straight and close, with moderate feathering. Liver and white or black and white, with or without tan markings.

HEIGHT

About 51 cm (20 in).

HEAD

Fairly broad and rounded, with a definite brow. Broad, medium-length muzzle and strong jaws. Medium-sized dark hazel eyes. Long, low set ears hanging close to the head.

NECK

Muscular and of a good length, broader towards the shoulders.

BODY

Compact and strong, with a deep chest and muscular, slightly arched loin.

LEGS

Well-muscled and strong in proportion with the body. Compact, round feet.

TAIL

Carried low, lightly feathered. Has traditionally been docked.

GROUP

Gundog (KC, ANKC). Sporting (AKC).

Probably the oldest of the spaniels and a larger, more solid dog than either the English or the American Cockers, the Springer was bred to 'spring' forward to drive game from its cover. It soon developed a range of gundog skills and is capable of pointing, hunting in thick woods or retrieving birds from ponds or marshes. Although it has been a recognized show breed and a pet for nearly 100 years, the English Springer and its smaller Welsh cousin remain essentially working dogs, virtually tireless on land or in water. The weatherproof coat makes this a hardy breed that is ready to accompany you anywhere at any time.

The English Springer has a distinctive gait, with the forelegs swinging straight forward from the shoulder. This makes for an easy, pacing stride, quite different from the eager busyness of the Cocker and giving the Springer an air of confidence.

Like most spaniels, the English Springer is friendly, obedient, eager to please and very fond of children. Its boundless energy can be kept to acceptable levels by consistent firm handling. Being a working dog, it needs plenty of exercise; denied this, it will run to fat and may develop eczema.

Irish Water Spaniel

The richly coloured and densely curled coat of the Irish Water Spaniel contains a natural oil which acts as an effective water repellent.

Water retrievers go back 1000 years or longer in Ireland, and this distinctive wildfowler would have been familiar as a type long before the breed as we know it appeared in the mid-19th century. The true breeding of the Irish Water Spaniel certainly indicates that it has been isolated for a long time without the infusion of foreign blood. Essentially it remains a working dog, recovering wildfowl and game over marshes, lakes and rough country.

The tallest of the spaniels, it is an agile, powerful swimmer, its oily coat protecting it from harsh conditions. Courage and loyalty are strong characteristics and it responds intelligently to firm training and socialization. Daily grooming is essential to keep the ringlet coat and hairy feet free of mats and mud, and it needs plenty of exercise. As long as these basics are attended to it makes an affectionate and good-natured pet.

CARE TIP

All dogs with pendulous, hairy ears can suffer from ear problems if they are not regularly checked and cleaned. It is not difficult to apply veterinary eardrops when infection or infestation does occur, and unless there is very painful inflammation a regularly handled dog will sit quietly while drops are applied.

COAT

Dense, tight, crisp ringlets with a natural oiliness, short on the face, muzzle and end of tail. A rich, dark liver colour.

HEIGHT

Dog: 53-58 cm (21-23 in); bitch: 51-56 cm (20-22 in). Slightly larger in North America.

HEAD

Comparatively broad, long skull; long, strong, squarish muzzle; distinct stop. Small, intelligent, amber eyes. Very long ears, lobe-shaped and pendulous.

NECK

Powerful, long and arched, set into sloping and powerful shoulders.

BODY

Short with deep, barrel-shaped rib cage.

LEGS

Rather long and strongly boned. Large, round feet.

TAIL

Distinctive, quite short and straight, thick at the root and tapering. Curls stop at about 7-10 cm (3-4 in) from the base.

GROUP

Gundog (KC, ANKC). Sporting (AKC).

Golden Retriever

This affectionate, gentle dog has earned a very good reputation for its relaxed behaviour with children. Its retrieving instincts remain strong even when the only 'game' it retrieves and carries gently in its soft mouth is its owner's carpet slippers or the daily paper.

COAT

Wavy and glossy with generous feathering. Cream to golden in colour.

HEIGHT

Dog: 56-61 cm (22-24 in); bitch: 51-56 cm (20-22 in).

HEAD

Broad with a good stop and wide, strong muzzle. Dark brown eyes set well apart. Medium-length ears.

NECK

Muscular and of good length.

BODY

Powerful and muscular with good symmetry and deep, well-sprung ribs.

LEGS

Strong, not too long, with round feet.

TAIL

Straight and feathered.

GROUP

Gundog (KC, ANKC). Sporting (AKC).

All Golden Retrievers are descended from litters bred by Lord Tweedmouth in Scotland in the mid-19th century, almost certainly from local wavy-coated retrievers and spaniels – although there is another story that he developed the breed from performing Russian shepherd dogs which so impressed him when he saw them in a circus that he bought the whole troupe.

Hardy, obedient, gentle and friendly, this breed has rightly earned its place as a favourite family dog, while still retaining its popularity as a gundog. It is one of the principal breeds used as guides for the blind.

Regular grooming with some attention to its feet plus plenty of exercise are all the Golden Retriever needs. It is happiest with companions, whether canine or human.

The universal popularity of this breed has unfortunately put heavy pressure on breeding stock and allowed a handful of unsound animals to pass on some serious faults both in temperament and physique. Prospective owners should take particular care when selecting puppies, buying only from a reputable breeder.

CARE TIP

A large, wet, muddy, hairy dog is better kept away from car upholstery and a mesh barrier is a prudent safety measure when transporting any dog. Whether ready-made or home-constructed, this is a sensible investment for all dog owners with cars.

Labrador Retriever

◀ *This affectionate, hardy sporting dog loves water and cool temperatures. Its dense, short coat comes in three colours, black, yellow to golden and liver, and provides protection in harsh conditions.*

The Labrador Retriever originated from dogs brought to Britain by Newfoundland fishermen who used them to retrieve their nets from the water. Their general hardiness both on land and in water, their soft mouths and scenting ability were immediately appreciated by sportsmen who later broadened the limited stock lines by introducing other sporting breeds of water spaniels and retrievers. The breed was well-established in Britain by the end of the 19th century, by which time it had ceased to be popular in Newfoundland: a local dog tax and the introduction of strict quarantine laws in Britain presumably meant that breeding Labradors ceased to be profitable. Today the Labrador Retriever is Britain's most popular gundog, as well as one of the most loved family dogs. In the domestic environment it is gentle, quickly trained and friendly. It will run to fat if not well-exercised.

Overbreeding, however, has created problems in some lines and care must be taken to ensure puppies are acquired from both physically and temperamentally sound stock. Avoid puppies that show any signs of nervousness or a tendency to snap.

COAT

In two layers, with a short, hard top coat and dense, waterproof undercoat. Black, yellow or other whole colours.

HEIGHT

Dog: 56-57 cm (22-22½ in); bitch: 54-56 cm (21-22 in). May be up to 62 cm (24½ in) in North America.

HEAD

Broad, clean cut skull with pronounced stop and strong, medium-length jaws. Medium-sized, brown or hazel eyes. Ears hang well back.

NECK

Powerful.

BODY

Strongly built and close coupled with deep, wide chest.

LEGS

Straight, well-boned with hocks, slightly bent on the hindquarters. Well-arched toes on round, compact feet.

TAIL

An 'otter tail', sturdy and well-covered, with short, dense hair. Medium-length, thick at base with gradual taper.

GROUP

Gundog (KC, ANKC). Sporting (AKC).

Weimaraner

The Weimaraner demonstrates balance, smooth co-ordination and stamina when it moves over the ground at speed. ▶

COAT

The short-hair has a fine sleek coat; in the long-hair it is up to 5 cm (2 in) long and carries feathering on the tail and legs. Usually a silvery metallic grey.

HEIGHT

Dog: 61-69 cm (24-27 in); bitch: 56-63 cm (22-25 in).

HEAD

Longish with a moderate stop, prominent occipital bone, and powerful jaw. The wide-set, intelligent eyes are blue-grey or amber, and the ears are broad and slightly folded.

NECK

Fairly long with clean lines.

BODY

Well-balanced, strong, with deep chest and well-sprung ribs.

LEGS

Strongly muscled with moderately angulated hindquarters. Firm, compact feet.

TAIL

Strong and tapering; in many countries it is still traditionally partially docked.

GROUP

Gundog (KC, ANKC). Sporting (AKC).

This distinctive, purpose-bred sporting dog was developed in Germany in the 18th century, but was not generally appreciated elsewhere until the middle of the 20th century when the British and the Americans 'discovered' this good-looking 'Silver Ghost'. Bred to find, point, track and retrieve both large and small game it carries the genes of the old St Hubert Hound, the Bloodhound and European Pointers in its blood. Its unusual silver-grey coat makes it easily recognizable, and, although the short-hair is more popular, there is also a long-haired variety.

The Weimaraner is intelligent, fearless, very obedient when firmly trained, and, if you choose your puppy from docile stock and give proper attention to socialization during its formative years, it will make a good family dog. It likes to use its brain and to work, so requires a great deal of supervised exercise. Its coat is virtually trouble free, but this is not a dog that thrives if kept outdoors.

CARE TIP

All dogs should have a constant supply of water in a bowl used exclusively for that purpose. Check the bowl regularly, making sure your dog has enough water, especially in hot weather and after exercise. Change the water frequently to keep it fresh and clean. The amount a dog drinks varies according to breed and individual preference, and also depends on such factors as diet.

Pointer

◀ *A real aristocrat among sporting gundogs, the Pointer is an outstandingly handsome worker, companion and family dog.*

The origins of the classic lines that define this exceptional gundog are said to be Foxhound, Greyhound and, variously, Italian Pointer, Bull Terrier, Bloodhound, Setter and even Bulldog. Possibly developed in the East, and then brought to Spain via Italy, the Pointer was refined to its present standard in Britain at the end of the 19th century. Marking the position of game birds on the ground, it stands on the point in a rigidly held pose that is truly remarkable.

Beautifully proportioned and well-muscled, it has a distinctive head and a deep chest. Working pointers are often heavier than those bred from show strains.

Friendly and sociable, it is a good family dog, requiring light though regular grooming and a fair amount of hard exercise to maintain condition. As with all fine-coated dogs, the Pointer should be brushed down after muddy exercise, or put in a rough straw box in an outhouse to dry and afterwards having any potentially irritating mud spots rubbed off.

CARE TIP

Washable 'bean' or polystyrene chip cushions are available in many sizes. For large, loose-limbed dogs these provide a comfortable mattress whether they want to lie sprawling or curled up.

COAT

Fine and short, in black and white, liver and white, lemon and white, self colours and tri-colours.

HEIGHT

Dog: 63-69 cm (25-27 in); bitch: 61-66 cm (24-26 in). 53-61 cm (21-24 in) in North America.

HEAD

The medium-breadth skull is in proportion to the length of the fore face; the slightly concave muzzle gives the distinctive 'dish face'. Soft hazel or chestnut eyes with darkish rims. Slightly pointed, medium-length ears lying close to the head.

NECK

Muscular, longish and slightly arched.

BODY

Well-muscled, well-proportioned and deep chested, with long, sloping shoulders.

LEGS

Strong and straight. Well-knit, oval feet.

TAIL

Straight and tapering.

GROUP

Gundog (KC, ANKC). Sporting (AKC).

English Setter

This elegant, deceptively powerful dog has proved itself not only to be one of the most successful hunters of the wily woodcock but also a sociable, good-natured family pet.

COAT

Long, silky, slightly wavy, with feathering. May be white and black, orange or lemon and white, liver or chestnut and white, or tricolour – all with speckling or ticking.

HEIGHT

Dog: 65-68 cm (25½-27 in); bitch: 61-65 cm (24-25½ in). Slightly smaller in North America.

HEAD

Long and lean with pronounced occipital bone and stop; squarish muzzle. Gentle, dark hazel eyes. Moderately long, folded ears.

NECK

Clean and muscular.

BODY

Deep-chested, strong and muscular with rounded ribs.

LEGS

Strong and muscular with long thighs and well-rounded feet.

TAIL

Slightly curved, medium-length and well-feathered.

GROUP

Gundog (KC, ANKC). Sporting (AKC).

Descended from an ancient line of sporting dogs going back before the 14th century in Britain and Europe and originally called spaniels, these large gundogs were subsequently seen to be different both in physique and talent in the hunting field. Fast and hardy, they set the birds, flush and retrieve over wide, spacious terrain. The English Setter was developed by Edward Laverack in England in the mid-19th century, but today there is marked difference between the heavier, hardier field setter and the show dog.

Active, lively and intelligent, it is a good-natured companion needing fairly firm training to control exuberance, plenty of exercise, regular grooming and frequent checks on ears and feet.

The related Gordon Setter is pehaps even more talented on the hunting field. It has great stamina and can cope with long periods without water. Like the English Setter, it makes a loyal and even-tempered companion. It is a handsome dog with a slightly shaggy black and tan coat.

CARE TIP

Larger dogs take much longer to develop than smaller dogs. Too much hard exercise in the formative first couple of years can damage and distort young bones and joints.

Irish Setter

◄ *The outstanding colour of the Irish Setter is unique, and when this breed is worked in its natural environment over open moorland it makes an impressive sight.*

Although the Irish Setter is still treasured by sportsmen it has become much more popular as a show dog, and attained the ultimate accolade in Britain of becoming Crufts Supreme Champion in 1993. Perhaps not surprisingly, for its bright red, glossy coat, its elegant lines and its size, combined with a friendly ebullient nature, mark it out in any crowd.

The original Irish setter was red and white – and the Red and White Setter remains a popular breed, having been developed from European, Springer and Water Spaniels. Mid-19th century British and Irish breeders were responsible for the selective breeding that perfected the physique and colour of the Irish setter, then the demands of the show ring almost ruined the breed before common sense prevailed and the strength and qualities of the sporting dog were revived.

The Irish Setter is a restless, bouncy, friendly character and will make a good companion for those who understand its need for firm training and very extensive exercise when mature.

COAT

Medium-long, flat and shiny; long, silky feathering. Rich chestnut, occasionally marked with white.

HEIGHT

Dog: about 66 cm (26 in); bitch about 63 cm (25 in). In North America up to 69 cm (27 in) is acceptable.

HEAD

Long and lean with a moderately deep muzzle, stop and pronounced occipital protuberance with raised eyebrows. Hazel to dark, almond-shaped eyes. Moderately long ears folded close to the head.

NECK

Clean set, moderately long and muscular.

BODY

Muscular, balanced proportions, deep chest, well-sprung ribs, sloping shoulders.

LEGS

Long, muscular and powerful with small, firm, strong feet.

TAIL

Nearly straight, medium-length and tapering.

GROUP

Gundog (KC, ANKC). Sporting (AKC).

Dandie Dinmont Terrier

The Dandie Dinmont shares its ancestry with a number of other terriers. The silky top knot and mixture of harsh and soft hair are particularly reminiscent of the Bedlington (see page 45). ▶

COAT

In two layers, the top coat is long and crisp, the undercoat softer. The two accepted colours are still 'pepper' and 'mustard'.

HEIGHT

About 20-25 cm (8-10 in).

HEAD

Strong and muscular, with a broad skull, domed forehead, deep muzzle and strong jaw. The head is covered with silky hair, including a pronounced top knot. Large, round, wide-set eyes are hazel in colour. Tapering ears are set low.

NECK

Not long but very muscular for the size of the dog.

BODY

Long and strong, with deep chest.

LEGS

Short and muscular, set wide apart. Forelegs slightly shorter than hind legs. Round, well-padded feet.

TAIL

Shortish, with a curve rather than a curl. Broad at base, then broadening slightly before tapering to a point.

GROUP

Terrier.

Legend surrounds the ancestry of many dogs; the Dandie Dinmont is perhaps the only one whose origins can be described as fictitious! Dandie Dinmont is a character in Walter Scott's novel *Guy Mannering*; he has six small terriers, either mustard or pepper in colour, which go everywhere with him. Although Scott invented the name, he 'borrowed' the idea of the mustard and pepper dogs – in real life they were owned by one James Davidson, an 18th century farmer in the English/Scottish Border country.

Guy Mannering was published in 1815, but terriers resembling the Dandie Dinmonts had been known in the Borders for at least 100 years before then. Like many other terriers, they were bred to hunt foxes and badgers. Scott remarks on their intrepid temperament: 'They fear'd naething that ever cam' wi' a hairy skin on't.'

Now more commonly seen as an affectionate pet, the Dandie Dinmont still makes a fearless guard dog. It is wary of strangers, but devoted to its owner and to children. It has an independent streak verging on the stubborn, but respects firm handling.

CARE TIP

The Dandie Dinmont and other long-haired dogs should be groomed every day using a fine-toothed comb and a wire-bristled carder or brush. These remove dead hairs and promote healthy growth.

Border Terrier

◀ *Unspoiled by being bred as a pet and show dog, the Border Terrier remains hardy, courageous and loyal.*

This game little dog has been known in the Border country of England and Scotland for 150 years, where it was bred as a fox hunter. Its thick, double-layered coat enabled it to cope with bad weather, while its stamina, compact build, comparatively long legs and powerful bite all made it ideal for its purpose.

It was recognized by the Kennel Club in 1920, rather to the dismay of some of its admirers, who felt that showing the breed would mean sacrificing some of its tougher qualities. Happily, this has not proved to be the case; even though it is now more often kept as a pet, the Border Terrier remains remarkably fit and is capable of keeping up with horses and hounds. This does mean that for such a small dog it requires a surprising amount of exercise.

If you are able to supply this need, the Border Terrier makes a rewarding companion. It is good-natured, intelligent, adaptable and gets on well with people and other animals (providing you don't happen to keep a fox).

CARE TIP

There are numerous toys you can buy for your dog, but choose them carefully, making sure they are too big for the dog to swallow and that there are no sharp edges or loose bits which might be dangerous. All the retrieving breeds love chasing a ball, a rubber bone or anything you care to throw for them. Toys will also stop a dog becoming bored and destructive.

COAT

Thick, straight and harsh in texture, with a close undercoat. May be red, wheaten, grizzle and tan, or blue and tan.

HEIGHT

About 25 cm (10 in).

HEAD

Otter-like, but broader across the skull than this suggests. Short, strong muzzle and square jaw. The dark eyes have a keen expression. Small, V-shaped ears fold forward close to the side of the head.

NECK

Of moderate length.

BODY

Longish for the size of the dog, deep and narrow. Ribs carried well back. Strong loins.

LEGS

Straight forelegs, not too heavy. The standard uses one word to describe the hindquarters: 'racy'. Small, well-padded feet.

TAIL

Shortish, thick at base and tapering to a point. Set high on the body and carried high, but not curled over the back.

GROUP

Terrier.

Skye Terrier

The Skye's coat is its pride and joy and should be combed every day, with thorough grooming at least once a week. Because its hair tends to trail along the ground, it does pick up mud, but this can be brushed off when dry. ▶

COAT

A long, hard straight top coat over a shorter, woolly undercoat. The coat flows thickly and evenly over body and head. May be any whole colour with shading of the same colour.

HEIGHT

Ideally 25 cm (10 in); bitches may be slightly smaller.

HEAD

Long for the size of the dog, with a broadish skull, slight stop and strong muzzle and jaws. Long hair falling over brown, medium-sized, close-set eyes. The ears are usually erect.

NECK

Long for the size of the dog.

BODY

Long, with level back, deep ribcage, short loins and muscular hindquarters.

LEGS

Short and strong, with well-padded feet.

TAIL

Long and well-feathered, with a graceful curve. May hang down or be carried in line with the back.

GROUP

Terrier.

The Skye Terrier comes from the Scottish island whose name it bears. Despite its glamorous coat, which covers it so thoroughly that only its ears and muzzle appear as distinctive features, it was originally a hunting dog, bred to catch foxes, badgers and otters. It has been around for at least 400 years, which makes it one of the oldest of the Scottish breeds, but no one seems to know how it comes to look like it does.

The world's most famous Skye Terrier, Greyfriars Bobby, helped to make the breed legendary for its loyalty. According to one version of the story, this little dog is supposed to have spent twenty years at his master's grave in Greyfriars Cemetery in Edinburgh, except for a daily visit to the cafe where they had eaten together. He resisted all attempts by his master's friends to offer him a comfortable home. After Bobby's own death, a statue in his memory was erected nearby.

Fierce loyalty to its owner is certainly a characteristic of the Skye. This can lead to its being unfriendly with strangers and, although it is unlikely to start a fight with other dogs, it is not slow to defend itself when necessary. It needs a reasonable amount of exercise, but is small enough to live happily in a flat or apartment.

Norwich/Norfolk Terriers

Both Norwich (illustrated) and Norfolk Terriers are hardy little creatures, retaining the working qualities they were bred for. Nevertheless they are good with children and fun to have around.

These closely related English terriers were shown as one breed until 1964 in Britain and 1979 in the United States, when the Norfolk was granted separate status. Until then, the Norfolk had been considered the drop-eared version of the Norwich. In the United States a man named Frank Jones was largely responsible for developing the breed in the years following the First World War. The alternative name of Jones Terrier has fallen out of use, but may be found in early histories of the Norwich and Norfolk.

The breeds are descended from Cairn, Irish and Border Terriers, and, as their names suggest, they originated in East Anglia, where they were first bred in the 19th century to hunt foxes, badgers and rats. Small enough to worm their way into a foxhole or badger sett, they have the typically fearless terrier temperament that enabled them to deal with prey very much larger than themselves.

As pets, both the Norwich and the Norfolk are friendly, intelligent companions, well able to defend themselves but less likely to start a fight than many other terriers. Like many intelligent dogs, they quickly become bored and boredom can lead to mischief. The answer is to keep them occupied. They need a fair amount of exercise, but will live quite happily in towns provided they have regular runs in a park.

COAT

Straight and coarse, with a thick undercoat. Colours may be red, red wheaten, black and tan or grizzle.

HEIGHT

25 cm (10 in).

HEAD

Broad skull with a definite stop and strong, wedge-shaped muzzle. Prominent eyebrows and whiskers. The deep set, oval eyes are dark brown or black. Medium-sized, wide set, V-shaped ears fall forward in the Norfolk and stand erect in the Norwich.

NECK

Muscular and of moderate length.

BODY

Compact, with powerful shoulders and a short, level back.

LEGS

Short, straight and powerful. Round, well-padded feet.

TAIL

Thick at the base and tapering to a point, carried erect. Has traditionally been docked to half its original length.

GROUP

Terrier.

Australian Terrier

Bred for hard work, the Australian Terrier is a busy extrovert making it an ideal companion for anyone prepared to give it enough exercise. 

COAT

In two layers, with dense, harsh, medium-length top coat and shorter, softer undercoat. May be blue and tan or sandy or red.

HEIGHT

25 cm (10 in).

HEAD

Long for the size of the dog, with powerful muzzle and strong jaw. The flat skull has a soft, silky top knot. Small, dark eyes are set wide apart. The pointed ears are carried erect.

NECK

Long, strong, slightly arched.

BODY

Long for the height of the dog, sturdy with deepish chest, level back and strong loins.

LEGS

Forelegs straight; the hind legs have muscular thighs and well-bent stifles and hocks. Small, well-padded feet.

TAIL

Set high on body and carried erect; traditionally docked.

GROUP

Terrier.

Bred by Australian settlers to deal with rats, rabbits and snakes, the Australian Terrier has a number of British antecedents, and probably has Cairns, Skyes, Dandie Dinmonts, Yorkshire Terriers and Scottish Terriers in its make-up. The Aussie became established as an intrepid working dog in the middle of the 19th century. It made its first appearance at a show in Sydney in 1899, but was slow to achieve popularity elsewhere; the breed was not recognized in Britain until the 1930s.

The Australian Terrier makes a delightful pet as it is devoted to humans and particularly good with children, always being ready to play. It is also an excellent, if noisy, watchdog. Obedient and eager to please, it will nevertheless put up a strong fight against other animals, if required.

Like many small terriers the Aussie is energetic and needs plenty of exercise, but is small enough to live happily in a flat or apartment if you can make sure it has a run in the local park every day.

Scottish Terrier

◀ *The Scottish Terrier has an independent nature, but can also be playful and enjoys carrying a ball or stick. It has great stamina and its body is remarkably powerful for such a compact dog, but it will run to fat if it doesn't get sufficient exercise.*

A number of breeds were loosely described as the 'Scottish Terrier' until the standard for the breed we know today was established in the late 19th century. It is also sometimes known as the Aberdeen Terrier. Like all terriers, the Scottie was originally a working dog; it was bred to hunt foxes, badgers, rats and other vermin. Although regarded as a traditional Scottish dog, familiar in whisky advertisements, in fact the Scottie has long been popular in Canada and gained in status in the United States during the presidency of Franklin Roosevelt, who had one as a pet.

The Scottie's bushy eyebrows give it a dignified look that has been likened to that of a disapproving Church of Scotland elder, and the breed is generally aloof with strangers. It is also not the ideal companion for a young family. It has a strong, stubborn streak that needs consistent firm handling, and it requires plentiful exercise and frequent grooming. It is therefore not an easy pet for someone with little experience of dogs. But with the adults it knows, the Scottie is a devoted and entertaining companion.

COAT

Long, thick, wiry top coat over shorter, softer undercoat. May be black, wheaten or brindle.

HEIGHT

25-28 cm (10-11 in)

HEAD

Long enough to appear rather narrow; strong, with flat skull and slight stop. Prominent eyebrows and beard. Deep set, almond-shaped, dark brown eyes with an alert expression. Neat, erect, pointed ears.

NECK

Of medium length but powerful.

BODY

Deep chest; shortish, muscular back; deep, muscular loins. Very strong hindquarters for the size of the dog.

LEGS

Short and strong, with powerful thighs. Rather large, well-padded feet.

TAIL

Of medium length, carried erect and tapering towards the tip.

GROUP

Terrier.

West Highland White

The West Highland White's eager expression makes it one of the most appealing small dogs. In the course of 100 years its popularity has spread through Britain to Europe and North America. ▶

COAT

In two layers, with a harsh, straight outer coat and short, furry undercoat. All white.

HEIGHT

28 cm (11 in).

HEAD

Slightly domed, broadish skull with a shortish muzzle giving a rather square look to the head. Strong jaws. Medium-sized, dark eyes set wide apart under bushy eyebrows. Small, erect, pointed ears.

NECK

Muscular, thickening towards the shoulders.

BODY

Compact, with deep chest, level back and strong loins and hindquarters.

LEGS

Short and muscular. Feet in proportion to the size of the dog, round and well-padded.

TAIL

Of medium length, straight and erect, with no feathering.

GROUP

Terrier.

One of many small, tough terriers to originate in Scotland, the Westie is related to the Scottish Terrier, the Dandie Dinmont and the Cairn. A similar style of terrier has been known in Scotland for several centuries, but it is said that from about 1860 onwards Westies were deliberately bred white in order to distinguish them from their quarry after a favourite (darker coloured) dog was accidentally shot and killed by its owner in the course of a hunting expedition. Early Westies probably had longer legs than are usual today, to enable them to cope with the rough terrain of their native land.

The first Westies were shown under the unimaginative name of White Scottish Terrier, but West Highland White was adopted in the early 20th century.

The Westie has an excellent temperament for a pet – it is hardy and adaptable, and although protective of its family it quickly overcomes its natural suspicion of strangers. It is also one of the most affectionate of the terriers, a playful companion for children and always eager to please. It loves exercise and will not be deterred by bad weather.

Regular grooming maintains the coat in good condition, and in bad weather stripping is beneficial.

Jack Russell Terrier

◀ *Hugely popular despite being 'unofficial' for so long, the Jack Russell is an intelligent, eager little dog always ready for a run or a game.*

Parson Jack Russell was a minister with a passion for fox hunting. In the early 19th century he found a need for a terrier that was small enough to go to ground in pursuit of a fox, but had long enough legs and sufficient stamina to follow the hunt until the moment came for it to go into action.

Although the terrier he produced was extremely efficient and became immensely popular, it was only recognized by the Kennel Club in 1990 and has still not achieved full breed status in North America or Australia. The reason for this lies in the great variation in type and the consequent difficulty of applying a standard. There has also been a certain amount of inverted snobbery among Jack Russell owners who are unwilling to see their breed's hardy working qualities sacrificed on the altar of beauty.

As a pet, the Jack Russell is affectionate and energetic, requiring quite a lot of exercise for such a small dog. It will busy itself quite happily around the garden, but it will soon grow fat if not given a regular run. Even its most ardent admirers admit that it can also be remarkably stubborn. It makes a good guard dog, but is excitable and tends to yap.

COAT

May be smooth or rough coated, white with black or tan markings.

HEIGHT

At the withers there are two height ranges: up to 28 cm (11 in) and 28-38 cm (11-15 in).

HEAD

Strong boned, with powerful jaws.

NECK

Muscular.

BODY

Well-muscled, with a broad chest and straight back.

LEGS

Straight forelegs, well-bent hind legs and cat-like feet.

TAIL

Set on high and carried gaily.

GROUP

Terrier (KC).

Cairn Terrier

The Cairn's weatherproof coat needs regular brushing. Excessive feathering on the legs and tail and long hairs round the ears and belly should be trimmed. An unpretentious little dog that prefers a 'natural' look. ▶

COAT

In two layers, with a harsh outer coat and shorter, softer undercoat. Almost any colour except black, white or black and tan.

HEIGHT

28-31 cm (11-12 in). Smaller in North America.

HEAD

Small, with a broad skull, well-defined stop and short but powerful muzzle. Medium-sized, wide-set, hazel eyes under shaggy eyebrows. Small, erect ears.

NECK

Solid and of a good length for the size of the dog.

BODY

Sturdy, with deep ribs and strong loins.

LEGS

Of medium length with strong thighs. Small but well-padded feet, with the forefeet larger than the hind.

TAIL

Short.

GROUP

Terrier.

The Cairn originated in the Scottish island of Skye, and takes its name from the piles of stones which often mark grave sites or high points on Scottish hillsides. The little terrier was skilled at raising a fox or other vermin which might have gone to ground in a cairn.

Something like the modern Cairn existed as long ago as the 15th century, but the breed was only recognized in Britain and the United States in the early 20th century. For some years thereafter the offspring of Cairns and West Highland White Terriers were accepted as pedigree dogs, the darker coated being registered as Cairns and the lighter as Westies; this practice was abandoned in 1924 to prevent the distinction between the two breeds being lost. The Cairn is an intelligent, inquisitive dog and makes a friendly, fun-loving companion. Careful early training and socialization should deal with its tendency to be over-protective of its owner.

CARE TIP

Most dogs only need a bath once every few months. Small dogs can be bathed in a sink, using an ordinary detachable spray. Larger dogs need a full-sized bath, and a rubber mat is useful to prevent them slipping. Use warm – not cold or hot – water and a shampoo specially formulated for dogs. Rinse carefully, working backwards from the head, and dry the dog thoroughly as soon as you have finished.

Sealyham Terrier

◄ *Properly cared for, the Sealyham is one of the most elegant and eyecatching of breeds. The luxurious coat covers a remarkably tough little body.*

Welsh in origin, the Sealyham was bred in the 19th century to hunt badgers, foxes and otters. The story goes that a certain Captain Edwards of Sealyham, in Pembrokeshire, was dissatisfied with the available breeds of terrier. He probably crossed a Corgi with a Dandie Dinmont to achieve the desired size and courage, but left no complete records of his activities; the modern breed may include traces of the West Highland White, Wire Fox Terrier, Bull Terrier, Flanders Basset and the extinct Old English White Terrier. Edwards was above all determined that his new terrier should be tough – any puppy that showed the slightest sign of cowardice was immediately shot.

Whether or not this tale is true, the modern Sealyham is a courageous animal with a tendency to stubbornness. It also has the typical terrier willingness to fight at the slightest provocation. If these potential drawbacks are eliminated with firm, early training, the Sealyham makes a loyal and affectionate pet.

The handsome coat requies a lot of attention. The Sealyham should be brushed and combed every day to keep it looking neat and to remove any dead hair. Hand stripping, which should be done at least twice a year, is usually done by a professional; inexpert stripping can make a real mess.

COAT

In two layers, the top coat long and coarse, the undercoat softer and thick. White, and with or without markings on head and ears.

HEIGHT

Maximum 30 cm (12 in), slightly less in North America.

HEAD

Wide, slightly domed skull. Long, powerful muzzle. Round, medium-sized, dark eyes. Medium-sized, rounded ears hang down by the sides of the cheeks.

NECK

Longish, thick and powerful.

BODY

Of medium length with a deep chest and very powerful hindquarters for the size of the dog.

LEGS

Short and strong, with round, cat-like feet.

TAIL

Erect, though has traditionally been docked. Set high on the back so that hindquarters extend beyond it.

GROUP

Terrier.

Staffordshire Bull Terrier

Like many dogs originally bred to work or fight, the Staffordshire will quickly grow fat if it does not have plenty of exercise. ▶

COAT

Short and smooth. May be almost any colour except liver or black and tan.

HEIGHT

35-40 cm (14-16 in).

HEAD

Broad, short and deep, with pronounced cheek muscles and stop, and short muzzle. Round, medium-sized dark eyes. Medium-sized 'rose' ears, folding over and backwards with the inside visible.

NECK

Shortish but muscular.

BODY

Muscular throughout: broad chest, deep brisket, level back, short loin and powerful hindquarters.

LEGS

Forelegs straight and set wide apart. Hind legs muscular with well-bent stifles. Medium-sized, well-padded feet.

TAIL

Medium length, preferably straight and tapering to a point; set low on the body and carried low.

GROUP

Terrier.

Like the Bull Terrier (see page 49), the Staffordshire was bred for bull baiting and fighting and was particularly popular in the Black Country of central England – which includes the county of Staffordshire. It is almost certainly descended from the crossing of Bulldogs with terriers. Its squarish head and stocky build are still reminiscent of the Bulldog ancestry, but after dog fighting became illegal, it was bred more for the terrier qualities of tenacity and intelligence.

The fast response to aggression for which the Staffordshire was once prized has not been lost and it can be pugnacious with other dogs. Firm training from an early stage is essential, and the Staffordshire should always be kept under control whenever it is likely to meet other dogs. It needs lots of exercise to maintain its fine physique and to stop it getting bored. That said, it is loyal and affectionate with its owner and family and is renowned for its love of children. The American Staffordshire Bull Terrier is a larger dog than its British cousin.

CARE TIP

Although most dogs love chewing on bones, these can be dangerous. Never give a dog any bone that it could swallow or that will shatter into sharp pieces. Stick to large shin bones, preferably cooked. As an alternative, rubber chews are available in a variety of shapes and sizes. Rawhide bones may also help lessen teething trouble in puppies.

Fox Terrier

The Fox Terrier (Smooth illustrated) is by nature an energetic hunter. It will soon get bored if it does not have enough exercise, so it is probably a better pet for those who live in the country rather than town-dwellers.

A Fox Terrier was running with hounds in England by the end of the 18th century, but this was a generic name that covered almost any dog that went to earth. The distinction between the two modern breeds, that is, Wire and Smooth, arrived at the end of the 19th century, the difference being purely in the coat.

It was a Fox Terrier that sat on record labels, listening to His Master's Voice, but it is not clear whether this contributed to the breed's enormous popularity in the 1920s, or whether the dog was chosen because the breed was already so popular.

Nowadays usually regarded as a companion dog, the Fox Terrier nevertheless retains its terrier instincts and is completely fearless. You will never be plagued by rats or rabbits while this dog is around. Its readiness to defend itself or its family against any hint of a threat can be a problem and should be kept under control by early and firm training. It is a friendly, cheerful dog, good with children and ready to adapt to any environment, provided its family is near at hand.

CARE TIP

The Wire Fox Terrier needs to be 'stripped' every few months. Brush the dog first to remove dirt and loose, dead hair. Then remove excess hair, either by hand plucking or with a stripping knife. 'Sculpting' any dog's coat – to achieve the desired mane, beard, eyebrows and other features for show purposes – is best left to an expert.

COAT

In the Wire Fox Terrier, dense and wiry, with a softer undercoat. In the Smooth, straight, smooth and flat all over. Both breeds are mainly white with or without black, black and tan or (in the Wire Terrier only) tan markings.

HEIGHT

Dog: maximum 37 cm (15½ in); bitch slightly less.

HEAD

Flat skull, sloping downwards and roughly equal in length to fore-face. Slightly tapered muzzle. Round, dark, eyes. Small V-shaped ears.

NECK

Longish and muscular.

BODY

Long shoulders, sloping steeply down from the junction with the neck. Deep chest; short, level back.

LEGS

Front legs straight with very little sign of an ankle. Long, muscular thighs and well-bent stifles. Round feet.

TAIL

Set high and carried erect; traditionally docked.

GROUP

Terrier.

Bedlington Terrier

The Bedlington is a much tougher dog than its gentle appearance might suggest. It makes an excellent watchdog, and will defend its corner fiercely whenever the need arises.

COAT

Unique to the breed, thick, soft and woolly. Blue, liver or sandy, all with or without tan.

HEIGHT

About 41 cm (16 in).

HEAD

Narrow with long, tapering muzzle. Domed skull with silky topknot. Small, deep set, almost triangular eyes are wide apart. Medium-sized ears with tips covered by a pompom-like fringe of hair.

NECK

Long, wider towards the shoulders, at a sharp angle to the body, so head is held high.

BODY

Longish, flexible but muscular, with deep chest and brisket. Arched back and well tucked-up belly.

LEGS

Forelegs straight but with feet closer together than the shoulders. Hind legs stretch out behind the body, appearing longer than the forelegs. Long, hare-like, well-padded feet.

TAIL

Low set, of medium length, tapering to a point.

GROUP

Terrier.

To call the Bedlington a wolf in sheep's clothing would be unfair, but it is certainly a terrier in a lambswool coat. It was bred about 200 years ago in northern England. Its original purpose was to hunt rats in the tunnels of coal mines and this task was later broadened to include control of rabbits and other vermin.

The Bedlington is probably related to the Dandie Dinmont, but which the ancestor is and which the descendant is unclear. Certainly the earliest Bedlingtons (known as Rothbury Terriers) were stockier dogs, and the modern breed owes its elegant profile and remarkable turn of speed to later crossing with the Whippet.

Now that it is more commonly kept as a pet, the Bedlington retains the qualities that made it an efficient terrier: intelligence, curiosity and absolute loyalty to its family. It is very fond of children, but not generally tolerant of other dogs.

Like the Poodle, the Bedlington does not shed its coat, which may make it a good choice for those prone to allergies; it also gives you a better chance of keeping your furniture free of hair. Even so, the coat should be brushed every day and clipped about once every six weeks to keep it smart.

Manchester Terrier

The keen look in the Manchester Terrier's eye harks back to its sporting origins; this dog is still happiest careering around the countryside, but will adapt to town life if given plenty of exercise.

COAT

Short, smooth and shiny; black with tan markings.

HEIGHT

Dog: 40 cm (16 in); bitch: 38 cm (15 in). In North America a weight range of 5.5-7.25 kg (12-16 lb) or 7.25-10 kg (16-22 lb) is specified.

HEAD

Long, flat skull, tapering only slightly to a wedge-shaped muzzle. Small, dark, almond-shaped eyes. Small, V-shaped ears fold over above the top of the skull.

NECK

Longish, broader at the shoulders.

BODY

Short, slightly arched with loins lower than the shoulders and belly well tucked-up.

LEGS

Forelegs straight. Muscular thighs and well-bent stifles. Small, strong, rather hare-like feet.

TAIL

Set on the end of the arch of the back, short, tapering to a point.

GROUP

Terrier.

The Manchester Terrier, descended from the now extinct Black and Tan Terrier and the Whippet, was developed in and around Manchester in the 19th century to control vermin. Rats and rabbits were its principal prey; in its heyday it was second to none as a hunter. It was also popular in the dubious sport of rat baiting, and its ears were often cropped to protect them from being damaged. Ear cropping was banned in Britain in 1895, however, and the natural, folded-over ears became standard.

An energetic, agile dog, the Manchester is an ideal companion for any active person. Friendly, clean and requiring minimum grooming, it makes a reliable family pet, though it does tend to be a one-person dog.

The English Toy Terrier, a separate breed in Britain, is shown in the United States as a toy version of the Manchester, hence the two weight ranges specified in the standard. The toy version became fashionable on both sides of the Atlantic at the end of the 19th century and this caused it a great deal of harm. Overbreeding and selection for the smallest possible size produced an alarming number of sickly animals. Fortunately, the fashion changed and the English Toy Terrier is once more a robust little dog.

Soft-Coated Wheaten

The Soft Coated Wheaten's luxurious coat belies its origins as a working animal. In addition to its farming duties, it was also used as a guard dog and for hunting. ▶

COAT

Soft and silky, wavy or loosely curly. 'A good, clean wheaten, a shade of ripening wheat' is the standard colour.

HEIGHT

Dog: 46-49 cm (18-19½ in); bitch slightly smaller.

HEAD

Flat, longish and rather wide, with well-defined stop and shortish, square muzzle. Abundant hair covering the entire head and falling down over the eyes. Medium-sized, dark hazel eyes under a strong brow. Thin, smallish, V-shaped ears hang down with the front edge close to the head.

NECK

Longish and muscular.

BODY

Compact, with long, muscular shoulders, deep chest, strong, level back and short loins.

LEGS

Straight, well-muscled forelegs; powerful thighs and hind legs. Strong, well-padded feet.

TAIL

Set high on the body and carried erect. Has traditionally been docked to a length of about 10-13 cm (4-5 in).

GROUP

Terrier.

It is possible to be reasonably definite about the ancestry of the Soft-Coated Wheaten: it is Irish, at least 200 years old and related to the Kerry Blue and the Irish Terrier. Its origins are surprisingly plebeian for such a luxuriously coated animal. In Ireland in the 18th century tenant farmers were forbidden by (English) law to own a dog worth more than five pounds, and the Soft-Coated Wheaten was cheap, ubiquitous and rather despised. In addition to its farming duties, it was used as a guard dog and for hunting; it has typical terrier sporting instincts.

Because of its lowly status, the Soft-Coated Wheaten took a long time to become established as a show dog. It was only recognized in Ireland in 1937; official acknowledgement in Britain, the United States and Canada came in the 1970s.

The Soft-Coated Wheaten is a cheerful, intelligent extrovert and makes a delightful companion. The only potential problem is a tendency to boisterousness, but as the Wheaten is always eager to please, patient training should keep this in check. Plentiful exercise is a must.

CARE TIP

Daily grooming is essential if the Soft-Coated Wheaten's abundant coat is to be kept clean and free of knots. A medium-toothed metal comb is best and will not make the coat frizzy. Trim any untidy long hairs on the ears, tail, feet and stomach.

Kerry Blue Terrier

Kerry Blue puppies are born black and take 18 months to acquire their full adult coat and colouring. Adults may be any shade of blue from silver to almost black.

The Kerry Blue is a descendant of the Irish Terrier and may have the Dandie Dinmont, the Bedlington and even the Irish Wolfhound in its ancestry. It was an established breed in Ireland before the Soft-Coated Wheaten, which is descended from it. The Kerry Blue was a multipurpose dog kept by Irish farmers for hunting, as a guard and to look after the herds. It is a good retriever on land or water, and a strong swimmer.

The name Kerry Blue became official in the 1920s, when the breed first appeared at Crufts and was introduced into the United States. Since then it has become popular in Canada and the Netherlands.

The Kerry is quite a demanding pet, requiring lots of exercise and frequent and thorough grooming. It also has a hearty appetite. Although affectionate and good with children, it has a stubborn streak and a fiery temper that will frequently get it into trouble unless this is controlled by firm, early training.

Preparing the Kerry Blue for showing is quite an art: the eyebrows are allowed to fall forward to the bridge of the nose, and the beard is kept long while hair on the rest of the head is short. Keeping the hair long on the underside of the body emphasizes the deep, powerful chest.

COAT

Abundant all over the body and legs, soft and silky with a slight wave. Blue, with or without black points.

HEIGHT

Dog: 46-48 cm (18-19 in); bitch: slightly smaller.

HEAD

Long and lean, with a flat skull, strong jaws and a beard. A long fringe falls over small dark eyes. Small, V-shaped ears.

NECK

Longish and muscular.

BODY

Flat shoulders, deep chest and brisket, level back and muscular hindquarters.

LEGS

Well-boned and well-covered in hair, giving a tubular effect. Small, round feet.

TAIL

Set high and carried erect. Traditionally docked.

GROUP

Terrier.

Bull Terrier

Beauty is certainly in the eye of the beholder so far as the Bull Terrier is concerned. But the breed has many admirers, and its devotion to its owner cannot be faulted.

COAT

Short and flat over a tight-fitting skin. White, when head may have coloured markings, or coloured, preferably brindle.

HEIGHT

About 53-56 cm (21-22 in).

HEAD

Long and strong, with an almost flat skull and tapering only slightly to the tip of the muzzle so as to appear egg-shaped from the front. Dark, narrow, triangular eyes. Small, erect ears are set quite close.

NECK

Longish and very muscular.

BODY

Broad, muscular shoulders. The short back slopes downwards from withers to loins and well-tucked-up belly forms a graceful curve on the underside.

LEGS

Strong and well-boned; hind legs have powerful thighs and well-bent stifles. Compact, round feet.

TAIL

Shortish, low set, broad at the base and tapering to a point. Carried no higher than level with the back.

GROUP

Terrier.

The ancestors of the Bull Terrier were fearless fighting dogs, probably the result of crossing Bulldogs and terriers. Although dog fighting, bear baiting and allied sports were outlawed in Britain in the early part of the 19th century, admirers of this type of dog nevertheless continued to breed it.

The Bull Terrier will fight to the death if necessary, and males in particular are innately hostile to other dogs. But in human company the breed is surprisingly docile, given its pugnacious history. It is affectionate, good with children and likes lots of attention. Normally a healthy dog, it will run to fat if it is not given plenty of exercise.

White Bull Terriers are often born deaf – have a puppy's hearing tested before you commit yourself to buying it. Variations in colour were introduced in the 1920s to combat this fault, and deafness does not seem to be so prevalent in coloured dogs.

CARE TIP

An improvised muzzle prevents a dog from biting. Tie a knot in the middle of a strip of bandage, then fold the ends over to form a loop. Slip the loop over the dog's muzzle with the knot at the bottom and pull it firm, but not too tight. Cross the two ends under the jaw and tie them together at the back of the neck.

Airedale Terrier

At least a daily brushing and, ideally, regular professional hand stripping are essential if the Airedale's coat is to be kept smart. Neglect this and your elegant terrier will soon turn into an unkempt woolly bundle.

The largest of the terriers, the Airedale was developed in Yorkshire in the mid-19th century. It was bred to be this size so that it could hunt badgers and otters, the most substantial animals terriers are called upon to deal with.

Endowed with great courage and stamina, excellent sight and hearing, the Airedale is a strong swimmer as well as a highly efficient hunter. It was much valued during the First and Second World Wars for its ability to locate the wounded and as a messenger and guard dog, although it was later superseded in these roles by other breeds such as the German Shepherd and the Dobermann.

After the Second World War the Airedale seemed to go out of fashion, but it is now enjoying a resurgence of popularity and is often found as a pet in Britain, Germany and North America. It is a loyal family dog, good with children and very protective of its owner. This last quality has occasionally got it into trouble: it is not usually the aggressor, but will react if provoked. Firm training from an early age is essential to keep aggression under control.

The Airedale is an eye-catching dog, although the coat requires a lot of attention. It is normal to leave a slight beard and bushy eyebrows on an otherwise neatly trimmed head.

COAT

Hard, wiry outer coat with a slight wave; softer undercoat. Tan, with the saddle, back of neck and top of tail either black or dark grey.

HEIGHT

Dog: 58-61 cm (23-24 in); bitch: 56-59 cm (22-23 in).

HEAD

Long, flat and narrowish. The forehead and muzzle make a continuous line. Powerful jaws. Small, dark, alert eyes. Smallish, V-shaped ears are set wide apart.

NECK

Longish and muscular, set at an angle so that the head is held high.

BODY

Compact, with short, level back and muscular loins.

LEGS

Straight and long for the size of the dog, well-covered with hair. Small, round feet.

TAIL

Set high on the body and carried erect. Has traditionally been docked so that the tip of the tail is level with the top of the skull.

GROUP

Terrier.

Lhasa Apso

The Lhasa Apso is an ideal pet, playful and affectionate. Independent by nature, it carries itself proudly and walks with a jaunty step. The only possible cause for concern is that it is wary of strangers, making early attention to socialization important. ▶

COAT

In two layers: long, straight, heavy top coat and fairly dense undercoat. It may be almost any colour from black to white.

HEIGHT

Dog: 25 cm (10 in); bitch: slightly smaller.

HEAD

Narrowish skull with moderate stop and medium-sized muzzle; the mass of hair makes the head seem larger than it is. Eyes dark, medium sized and oval, set well-forward. Pendulous, hairy ears.

NECK

Strong and hairy. Males have a pronounced mane.

BODY

Long for the size of the dog. Compact, with level back and strong loins.

LEGS

Straight and well-feathered. Round, cat-like feet.

TAIL

Plume-like, set high on the body and carried over the back. Often kinked.

GROUP

Utility (KC). Non-sporting (AKC, ANKC).

A hardy little dog from the mountains of Tibet, the Lhasa, also known as the Tibetan Apso, has a long, heavy, weatherproof coat and a fringe of hair over its eyes to protect it, perhaps, from the glare of sun and snow.

In its native land it has been known for many centuries as a pet and guard dog of the Tibetan monks; it took part in religious ceremonies and was thought to bring good luck.

The Lhasa did not reach the West until early in the 20th century. There is a suggestion that the dogs were smuggled out of Tibet, but it seems more likely that they were given as gifts to British officials in India. The first pair in the United States was certainly a present from the Dalai Lama.

The dogs quickly became popular as pets, and in the show ring the breed's reputation was enhanced by a Lhasa becoming Crufts Supreme Champion in 1984. Although the coat needs a lot of attention, the Lhasa is otherwise easy to look after as it does not need much to eat and requires little exercise.

CARE TIP

If your dog won't take liquid medicine from a spoon, use a syringe without a needle, available from your veterinary surgery. Simply lift the dog's upper lip, prise the teeth slightly apart if there is not a convenient gap in them, and squirt the liquid in.

Tibetan Spaniel

An ideal pet, easy to care for, reliable and good with children. The Tibetan Spaniel enjoys exercise and will dash round the garden in a most undignified manner before resuming its proud and independent air. Cool with strangers, it is loyal and affectionate with its family.

The Tibetan Spaniel has a haughty look that belies its fun-loving temperament and is rather like a large Pekingese in appearance.

This is another dog that originated in the monasteries of Tibet, where for many centuries it was used to turn prayer wheels, so that Buddhists who did not relish the exercise involved in such activity could still reap the spiritual benefits of this devout action. Whether the Tibetan Spaniel is an ancestor or a descendant of the Pekingese is open to question; it may also have been bred from a mixture of the Lhasa Apso and Japanese Chin.

As is the case with so many breeds, the Tibetan Spaniel's name is misleading – it is not a spaniel. It was first seen in Britain in 1905 and the name was probably chosen to distinguish it from the Tibetan Terrier which was becoming known at about the same time.

The Tibetan Spaniel has a particularly beautiful, gleaming coat which needs daily grooming; the dog will also benefit from a bath every few weeks. Other than that it is easy to care for and a joy to have around.

COAT

Longish, silky top coat with fine, dense undercoat in any colour or mixture of colours.

HEIGHT

25 cm (10 in).

HEAD

Small with slightly domed skull and slight stop. Blunt medium-length muzzle. Eyes are dark brown, oval, medium-sized and face forward. Medium-sized, well-feathered ears hang downwards.

NECK

Shortish but strong, enabling the head to be carried proudly. Males have a distinct mane.

BODY

Longish for the size of the dog, with a level back. Strong hindquarters.

LEGS

Forelegs slightly bowed; hind legs straight. Elongated, hare-like feet with feathering between the toes.

TAIL

Plume-like, and carried in a curl over the back.

GROUP

Utility (KC). Non-sporting (AKC). Toy (ANKC).

Shih Tzu

The Shih Tzu is rightly proud of its beautiful coat and likes to be admired. It loves human company, expects lots of attention and will soon let you know if it feels neglected. 

COAT

Very long and thick, wavy but not curly. May be any colour, but should ideally have a white forehead and tip to the tail.

HEIGHT

26-28 cm (10-11 in). A minimum of 20 cm (8 in) is accepted in North America.

HEAD

Broad, with a short, wide muzzle and upturned but not squashed nose. Well-covered with hair. Large, round eyes, usually dark. Long, drooping ears densely covered with hair.

NECK

Of moderate length, arched to enable the head to be carried proudly.

BODY

Long and sturdy for the size of the dog.

LEGS

Short but muscular. Round feet well-covered with hair, making them look big for size of dog.

TAIL

Heavily plumed with a curl near the base, carried jauntily over the back.

GROUP

Utility (KC). Toy (AKC). Non-sporting (CKC, ANKC).

While the alternative name of Chrysanthemum Dog may not sound very dignified, Shih Tzu literally means 'lion dog'. It was both guard dog and pet at the imperial court in China for many centuries, and at one time was even considered sacred. Its name refers both to the mane-like hair and to its legendary courage.

The Chinese were very protective of their revered dog, with the result that the Shih Tzu was not introduced into Britain or the United States until the 1930s. It was briefly categorized with the Lhasa Apso (to which it is related) by the Kennel Club, but the two breeds now have separate status.

The Shih Tzu makes a delightful pet, extrovert and enthusiastic. It loves luxury and needs only a moderate amount of exercise. It is good with children and devoted to its family, but tends to be aloof with strangers. Like any long-haired dog, the Shih Tzu can get into a terrible mess if not groomed frequently. Brush daily, keep the hair out of the eyes to lessen the risk of infection and check the ears regularly.

CARE TIP

Grooming a small- to medium-sized dog is easier if you put it on the table. It also helps to avoid confusing your dog: the floor is where the dog plays, so if you also make it a grooming area the dog may not realise it is required to stand still. A rubber grooming mat will stop the dog skidding about and is aesy to keep clean.

French Bulldog

◄ *Like its British relative, the French Bulldog is a courageous and intelligent animal. It is very playful and thrives on human companionship.*

When bull baiting was made illegal in Britain in the 1830s, less aggressive Bulldogs became popular as pets. The breed was common in the Midlands where lacemaking was an important craft. During the course of the 19th century, many lacemakers emigrated to France in search of better jobs and took their pets with them. Interbreeding produced a much smaller dog with slightly different features, notably the distinctive bat ears. Thus the French Bulldog was born. Or so one story goes. Alternatively, the smaller, bat-eared version of the Bulldog may have been bred in Spain as a bull fighter and imported into France.

Certainly the *Bouledogue Français* was fashionable by the end of the 19th century in both Britain and the United States, and the French Bulldog has remained popular. It is an affectionate, lively, and intelligent dog, fun with children and quietly devoted with the elderly. It has one great advantage over its larger cousin in that it is not prone to breathing problems.

However, the folds of skin on its face can cause irritation, just as they can on any loose-skinned dog. Rubbing in a little petroleum jelly will help prevent this. It also dislikes the heat and may suffer from sunstroke, so *never* leave it in a car that is likely to get hot.

COAT

Short, fine and glossy. May be brindle, with or without white markings, pied (in which case white predominates) or fawn.

HEIGHT

About 30 cm (12 in).

HEAD

Square and broad with well-defined stop and broad, deep muzzle. Loose skin forms wrinkles on the forehead and muzzle. Very short nose and overhanging upper lips. Medium-sized, upright, bat ears, rounded at the top. Dark, wide set eyes low on the skull.

NECK

Thick and powerful, with loose skin at the throat.

BODY

Short, strong and broad, with a deep brisket, wide shoulders and narrow loins.

LEGS

Forelegs short, straight, muscular and set wide. Hind legs a bit longer. Small, compact feet.

TAIL

Very short and low set, tapering to point. Straight or kinked.

GROUP

Utility (KC). Non-sporting (AKC, ANKC).

Bulldog

Do not judge a dog by its appearance. This ugly and pugnacious-looking creature makes an intelligent, gentle and loving pet. It is easy to look after, requiring minimal grooming and only moderate exercise.

COAT

Short, smooth and fine. May be brindle, red or fawn, with or without white markings, or all white or black and white.

HEIGHT

About 30-35 cm (12-14 in).

HEAD

Large, broad and square. Short, broad, deep muzzle with loose, wrinkled skin. The thick chops overhang a very broad lower jaw. Round, dark eyes are set low. Small ears are high on the head.

NECK

Shortish, thick and strong, with folds of loose skin.

BODY

Very powerful shoulders and deep brisket. Strong, broad back.

LEGS

Very strong and stout, especially the forelegs. The hind legs are slightly longer. The forefeet turn out slightly.

TAIL

Shortish, set on low, thick at base but tapering to a point. May be straight or 'screw'.

GROUP

Utility (KC). Non-sporting (AKC, ANKC).

Long associated with that legendary symbol of Britishness, John Bull, the Bulldog is supposed to reflect the characteristics of the British nation: honesty, strength, determination and courage in the face of adversity. It was, of course, the British who drew these parallels and declared the Bulldog to be the 'national dog'.

The breed's original purpose was less admirable – it was bred for bull-baiting as long ago as the 13th century and probably shares fighting ancestors with the Boxer and the Mastiff. Bull-baiting became illegal in the 1830s, but by that time the Bulldog's quintessential Britishness had become established and the dog continued to be bred. A wave of popularity in New York early in the 20th century helped to establish the Bulldog in the United States.

Bulldogs are affectionate dogs, playful and good with children. Owners should, however, be aware of the potential problems caused by the characteristic squashed nose. Overbreeding has tended to exaggerate these problems, so it is particularly important to choose a bulldog puppy from sound stock. The Bulldog cannot breathe rapidly and so should not be allowed to become overheated. Always make sure that it has access to cool shade and plenty of air if you leave it in the car. It also tends to drool, but this can be treated if the drooling becomes excessive.

Tibetan Terrier

◀ *Not unlike a miniature Old English Sheepdog in appearance, the Tibetan Terrier has many of that breed's steady qualities.*

The Tibetan or Lhasa Terrier is an ancient breed and probably the ancestor of the Lhasa Apso and Shih Tzu. The most plausible version of its history is that it was bred as a herder, working in tandem with the much larger Tibetan Mastiff which guarded the herds. Less hardy individuals were given to the Tibetan monks, who in turn may have given them to nomadic tribes to protect them on their travels; it is also possible that the nomads stole the dogs, but this would surely have brought them bad luck. Another account claims that the Tibetan Terrier originally came from Japan and was brought to Tibet by nomadic traders. Whatever the truth may be, it is a herding dog, not a terrier.

Like the other Tibetan dogs now popular in the West, the Tibetan Terrier has a long and luxurious coat. Typically it has a fringe falling forward over the eyes, a small beard and a jaunty kink to its tail.

It makes an excellent guard and has a powerful, siren-like bark surprising in a dog this size. It is also a loyal and affectionate pet, though it has a mind of its own and needs firm training. Although its coat requires regular grooming, it does not need a great deal of exercise. This is a playful breed and will enjoy human company in the garden or the occasional foray into the countryside.

COAT

Abundant but fine, long top coat which may have a slight wave and a woolly undercoat. Any colour except chocolate or liver.

HEIGHT

Dog: 35-40 cm (14-16 in); bitch: slightly smaller.

HEAD

Medium sized with definite stop and strong muzzle. Covered with long hair. Large, round, dark brown eyes. V-shaped, pendant ears, heavily feathered.

NECK

Short, but allowing the head to be held jauntily.

BODY

Compact and muscular. Level back and slightly arched loins.

LEGS

Profusely covered with hair. Forelegs straight; stifles well bent. Large, round feet well covered with hair, including between the toes and pads.

TAIL

Medium-length, well feathered and carried curled over back.

GROUP

Utility (KC). Non-sporting (AKC, ANKC).

Poodle

The traditional 'lion cut' illustrated here on a Standard Poodle is still favoured in the show ring. Away from shows, many owners of Poodles prefer to keep the coat well clipped but a uniform length all over.

COAT

Copious and harsh in texture, with a distinctive curl. It may be any solid colour.

HEIGHT

Standard: over 38 cm (15 in); Miniature: 11-15 cm (28-38 in); Toy under 28 cm (11 in) but 25 cm (10 in) in North America.

HEAD

In proportion to size of dog. Long, with a moderate stop and finely chiselled muzzle. Dark, almond-shaped eyes. Long, wide, pendulous ears.

NECK

Longish and strong.

BODY

Strong shoulders and deep chest; short, strong back.

LEGS

Muscular; forelegs are set very straight on the body. Smallish, oval feet with arched toes and thick pads.

TAIL

High set. Usually docked.

GROUP

Utility (KC). Non-sporting (AKC, ANKC).

Originally the Poodle was probably a German water dog – its name is connected with 'puddle' – and it is an excellent retriever both in and out of water. Its French name, *caniche*, is probably related to the word for duck, *canard*, reaffirming the water/hunting connection.

This is an intelligent, playful breed that is easy to train and which loves to show off; these qualities and its stylish appearance made it a great crowd-puller in 19th century French circuses. It was already fashionable as a pet, having been a favourite of Marie Antoinette, and its popularity has never waned.

The Miniature and Toy Poodles are more recent developments – their tempers are less reliable than that of the Standard Poodle and they may be nervous with children. But they make intelligent and affectionate pets, and, when carefully selected, are generally very hardy.

An interesting feature of Poodles is that they do not shed their hair. This may make them a good investment for people who are normally allergic to dogs, but do check with your medical advisor that dog hair is the cause of your allergy. Frequent brushing and combing will keep the coat in condition and regular clipping will make the job easier and keep the dog cooler in hot weather.

Boston Terrier

The Boston Terrier's erect ears are more like those of the French than the English Bulldog. The breed continued to develop after it was first established, and a typical modern Boston Terrier is less chunky in appearance than it would have been 100 years ago.

The Boston Terrier, or Round Head, is probably more Bulldog than terrier, but it was certainly bred in Boston. It was originally known by the more descriptive name of American Bull Terrier, but this aroused hostility among breeders of the already established (English) Bull Terrier. The Boston Terrier was recognized by the American Kennel Club in 1893. By the 1920s it was wildly fashionable throughout the United States where it is still a very popular breed and its qualities are increasingly being acknowledged around the world.

Like the Bulldog and the Bull Terrier, the Boston Terrier was bred for fighting – in this case primarily dog fighting – but is now most commonly kept as a pet. Lively, intelligent and boisterous, it is also obedient and responds well to training. It loves human company and games, and is good with children.

Boston Terriers are not very hardy and should not be kept in outdoor kennels. They are prone to breathing problems, so should not be allowed to become overheated.

CARE TIP

Take great care if you trim your dog's nails yourself. Hold the dog's foot firmly but gently and use clippers which will give a clean cut. It is important not to cut the quick, as this will bleed and hurt the dog. The quick is usually visible in clear nails, but dark nails are more difficult.

COAT

Short, smooth and glossy. Brindle with white markings is the preferred colour combination.

HEIGHT

About 38-43 cm (15-17 in).

HEAD

Square, flat-skulled, with short, square, deep muzzle and square jaws. Large, dark, wide-set eyes with an alert expression. Small, thin ears carried erect, sometimes cropped in the United States.

NECK

Longish and gracefully arched.

BODY

Deep chest and ribcage, sloping shoulders, short back and short muscular loins.

LEGS

Straight forelegs quite wide apart; muscular thighs.

TAIL

Short, without fringes, tapering to a point. May be either straight or screw.

GROUP

Utility (KC). Non-sporting (AKC, ANKC).

Shar Pei

The Shar Pei may look worried and slightly comical, but it has an affectionate disposition and a calm outlook on life. ▶

COAT

Short and bristly, creamy fawn, red or black.

HEIGHT

41-51 cm (16-20 in). A minimum of 46 cm (18 in) is demanded in North America.

HEAD

Largish and broad with moderate stop and loose, wrinkly skin. Longish, broad muzzle. Padded lips and blue-black tongue. Almond-shaped eyes. Small, triangular, wide-set ears with tips folded over.

NECK

Short and strong, with wrinkles on the underside.

BODY

Deep, broad chest with muscular shoulders; short, strong back and loins; muscular hindquarters.

LEGS

Strong, straight, fairly long.

TAIL

Base broad and round, tapering to point. Carried high, curved over the body.

GROUP

Utility (KC). Non-sporting (AKC, ANKC). Not recognized in Canada.

Although it has a long history, having been known as a guard and working dog in China more than 2000 years ago, the Shar Pei, or Chinese Fighting Dog, has only recently become familiar to dog lovers worldwide. In the 1940s the newly established People's Republic of China increased the tax on dogs so that few people could afford to keep them and those that served no useful purpose were slaughtered. The Shar Pei, at that time barely known outside its native land, very nearly became extinct.

The enthusiasm of one dedicated Californian breeder contributed a great deal to its survival, but as recently as 1980 the Shar Pei featured in the *Guinness Book of Records* as the rarest dog in the world. It is currently growing in popularity and becoming a familiar breed in Europe: in Italy it may be seen curled up under a market stall, oblivious to the activity going on around it. But breeding from limited stock has exaggerated faults in the Shar Pei's temperament, notably a tendency to aggression. Prospective owners should be particularly careful to choose a puppy from sound stock and a reputable breeder.

Shar Pei puppies seem to have lots of excess skin, but grow into their coats as they mature. Very loose skin is considered a fault in adults, but the wrinkles on the face contribute to the frowning expression which is part of this dog's appeal.

Keeshond

◀ *Active, intelligent and hardy, the Keeshond makes a friendly companion for young or old, though it tends to be a one-person dog.*

The Keeshond is the Dutch national dog and has worked on the barges of Amsterdam for several hundred years. Its ancestors probably came south with the Vikings. According to legend, the port of Amsterdam was founded by a Viking chieftain who had been rescued from drowning by a Dutch fisherman and his dog. A dog, Keeshond-like in appearance, appears on the Amsterdam coat of arms, and carrying a dog on board ship has always been a good omen for the Dutch bargees. The animals also earned their keep by controlling vermin and guarding the ships.

The name 'Keeshond' (pronounced Kayshond) means, simply, 'Kees's dog'. Kees was Cornelis de Gyselaer, who led a successful revolt against the ruling House of Orange in the 18th century. The popular barge dog became the symbol of his movement. Owning a Keeshond became politically unwise when the House of Orange returned to power, and the more neutral name of Dutch Barge Dog became current.

The Keeshond requires plenty of exercise and regular but not too strenuous grooming. It makes a good house dog, but firm and early training is recommended to control its tendency to bark and to keep its natural exuberance within bounds.

COAT

In two layers, with a harsh, straight top coat and a softer, undercoat. Prominent ruff. Grey or black topcoat, with cream or light-grey undercoat, markings and legs.

HEIGHT

Dog: 46 cm (18 in); bitch: 43 cm (17 in). In North America 49 cm (19 in) is permitted.

HEAD

Medium sized, with a flat skull, definite stop and wedge-shaped muzzle. Dark, medium-sized eyes, obliquely set, with markings giving the appearance of spectacles. Small, erect, velvety ears.

NECK

Longish, well-arched with dense hair.

BODY

Compact with deep brisket, shortish back and powerful hindquarters.

LEGS

Strong, straight, and feathered. Largish, padded, cat-like feet.

TAIL

Set high; longish and carried in a tight curl over the back.

GROUP

Utility (KC). Non-sporting (AKC, ANKC).

Schnauzer

It takes quite a lot of work to maintain the Schnauzer's sleek appearance. The body hair should be combed and clipped, and the beard and long hair on the ears and legs needs regular trimming to keep it smart. ▶

COAT

Short and wiry with a thick undercoat, either black or 'pepper and salt'.

HEIGHT

Comes in three sizes (see text). The popular Standard is: dog: 48 cm (19 in); bitch: 46 cm (18 in).

HEAD

Broad with moderate stop and longish muzzle. Prominent eyebrows, moustache and beard. Dark, oval eyes. Smallish ears fold forwards.

NECK

Longish, strong and slightly arched.

BODY

Broad, deep chest; broad, straight back sloping downwards to sturdy loins.

LEGS

Forelegs and thighs straight; hind legs from stifle to hock stretch out behind body.

TAIL

High set, has traditionally been docked.

GROUP

Standard and Miniature: Utility (KC). Giant: Working (KC). All sizes: Working (AKC), Utility (ANKC).

Available in three sizes – Giant, Standard and Miniature – the Schnauzer is a lively and loyal companion, fond of children and a good house dog. Be warned, though, that even the Miniature needs a lot of exercise, and with all Schnauzers the coat needs careful, daily attention. They are prone to skin diseases if kept in too warm a house.

The Standard (usually just called the Schnauzer in Britain) is the oldest of the three varieties, having been known in Germany as a herder, coach dog and efficient hunter of rats for hundreds of years. The Giant and Miniature Schnauzers became official in the early years of this century, and all Schnauzers are now popular the world over. The Giant Schnauzer is a large and solid dog, ranging in height from 60-70 cm (23½ -27½ in), while the Miniature is 33-35 cm (13-14 in).

Perhaps because of its convenient size, the Miniature is the favoured family pet, but it does tend to bark. In country areas the Giant Schnauzer is still a useful working dog. Schnauzers do tend to be wary of strangers, so early training is very important.

CARE TIP

A dog and cat brought up together in the same household will learn to live with each other – that may mean ignoring each other and taking pains not to encroach on each other's space, or it may mean they become the best of friends.

Chow Chow

◀ *Although the Chow is one of the most gorgeous of dogs, keeping its coat in good condition is not an onerous task: a quick going over every day, together with a full scale groom once a week (twice in the moulting season), is quite sufficient.*

The evidence of Chinese art attests that the Chow existed in China at least 2000 years ago, and that even in those days it looked very like the modern breed. Indeed, the earliest skeletons of dogs found anywhere in the world, thought to be several million years old, resemble the Chow.

With its lush coat and characteristic stiff-legged walk, the Chow does not look very primeval, neither does it look much like a guard dog, a hunter or a hard-working draught animal – it has, however, earned its keep in China for centuries performing all these tasks. It has been kept for its fur and even eaten as a delicacy – the word 'chow' is Cantonese for food.

It was imported into Britain in the 18th century and displayed in a zoo as the 'Wild Dog of China'! Queen Victoria helped make the Chow popular as a pet and it has been an established breed on both sides of the Atlantic for 100 years.

Although aloof with strangers and not altogether reliable with unknown children, the Chow is incomparably loyal to its owner. By nature a one-person dog, it can be an affectionate family pet, but still tends to attach itself most to the individual of its choice.

COAT

Coarse top coat and soft, woolly undercoat. Thick mane and 'breeches' on hind-quarters. Colours: black, blue, red, fawn, cream or white.

HEIGHT

Dog: 48-56 cm (19-22 in); bitch: 46-51 cm (18-20 in). In North America 51 cm (20 in) is the maximum for both sexes.

HEAD

Flat skull, medium-length muzzle and strong jaws. Bluish-black tongue. Smallish, dark, almond-shaped eyes. Small, thick ears.

NECK

Powerful and slightly arched.

BODY

Muscular with powerful shoulders, deep chest and strong hindquarters.

LEGS

Straight, well-boned and hairy. Small, cat-like feet.

TAIL

Hairy and curled over back.

GROUP

Utility (KC). Non-sporting (AKC, ANKC).

Siberian Husky

Although the word husky is used as the generic name for any Arctic sled dog, the Siberian Husky is a specific and recognized breed. ▶

COAT

Very thick. In two layers, with a straight top coat and a softer inner coat, shed in spring. May be any colour.

HEIGHT

Dog: 53-60 cm (21-24 in); bitch 51-56 cm (20-22 in).

HEAD

In proportion to the size of the dog. Slightly domed skull, distinct stop and longish, tapering muzzle with strong jaws. Almond-shaped blue or brown eyes set obliquely. Triangular ears set high on the head and carried erect.

NECK

Strong and well-arched.

BODY

Muscular shoulders, deep chest, level back and slim but powerful loins.

LEGS

Solid, strong, straight forelegs; hind legs have well-bent stifles. Oval, hairy feet.

TAIL

Brush-like; hangs low in repose but carried in a curl over back when dog is alert.

GROUP

Utility (KC, ANKC). Working (AKC).

A sled dog, similar to the Siberian or Arctic Husky, has been vital to the survival of the Chukchi people for thousands of years. Living in the barren wastes of Siberia and needing to travel long distances to hunt, they bred a dog with a modest appetite, extraordinary stamina and the ability to withstand temperatures as low as -50°C (-58°F). A team of huskies might number six or sixteen, depending on the load to be dragged. The Chukchi bred their dogs carefully, castrating all but the best of the lead males to ensure that only desirable characteristics were reproduced.

Introduced into North America early in the 20th century, the Husky was soon competing in winter sports; both lighter and faster than other popular Arctic breeds, it is still often used – and is extremely successful – in competitive sled racing.

The Siberian Husky's abundant coat is surprisingly trouble-free, but when it is moulting it should be groomed every day with a fine-toothed comb to remove excess hair. For the rest of the year a good brushing twice a week will suffice. It is an affectionate creature, good with children, and because it was bred for teamwork it is by nature tolerant of other dogs. But it needs a great deal of exercise and will easily become bored and wilful if this is neglected. Its characteristic wolf-like howl is a constant reminder of its wild origins.

Dalmatian

◀ *The Dalmatian is a friendly dog that likes human company. It needs lots of exercise and is therefore not a good choice for city dwellers who live in small buildings without access to parks. On the plus side, it needs very little grooming.*

The Dalmatian earned its alternative name Coach Dog in the early 19th century, when it was popular as a carriage dog in Britain and France. The Dalmatian will run alongside or under almost any vehicle and it became fashionable for the gentry to add these eye-catching dogs to their entourage when travelling with coach and horses. Dalmatians still show a remarkable affinity with horses.

The breed may have been introduced to Dalmatia in south-eastern Europe from India or the Middle East, or it may have originated in another part of Europe. Alternatively, it may have been given its name because it acted as a messenger in Dalmatia during the Balkan Wars in the early 20th century. All that seems to be certain is that the Pointer is one of its ancestors, and that the breed has been known for at least 300 years. Its popularity was greatly boosted in 1959 when Walt Disney made a delightful film of Dodie Smith's novel *The Hundred and One Dalmatians*.

Dalmatian puppies are born white. The spots which give the breed its distinctive and distinguished appearance begin to emerge after about two weeks, and the patterns continue to develop for the first year of the dog's life.

It is particularly important to buy Dalmatians from sound stock, as overbreeding when the breed was at the height of its popularity increased the risk of faults in soundness as well as temperament.

COAT

Short and glossy; white with well-defined spots of black or liver.

HEIGHT

Dog: 58-61 cm (23-24 in); bitch: 56-58 cm (22-23 in). As small as 48 cm (19 in) is permitted in North America.

HEAD

Longish and fairly broad with a flat skull and moderate stop. Long, powerful muzzle and strong jaws. Round eyes, dark in black-spotted dogs, amber in liver-spotted. Fine ears are carried close to the head.

NECK

Longish, broader at shoulders, well arched.

BODY

Deep, capacious chest, powerful, level back and slightly arched loins.

LEGS

Straight and well-rounded. Round, cat-like feet.

TAIL

Longish, tapering, with slight upward curve. Preferably spotted.

GROUP

Utility (KC). Non-sporting (AKC, ANKC).

Welsh Corgis

Both Pembroke (illustrated) and Cardigan Corgis make excellent pets, but they are primarily working dogs and need plenty of exercise. Deprived of a good daily outing they will quickly run to fat. ▶

COAT

Medium length, straight and thick. Cardigan: any colour except all white. Pembroke: red, sable, fawn or black and tan. Both breeds may have white markings.

HEIGHT

25-30 cm (10-12 in).

HEAD

Fox-like in shape, moderate stop and slightly tapering muzzle. Eyes are alert-looking; colour matches that of coat. Wide-set, erect ears.

NECK

Longish, muscular, fitting well into sloping shoulders.

BODY

Longish with level back. Body is slightly longer and chest less deep-set in Cardigan.

LEGS

Short, straight and muscular. Cardigan's feet are round, Pembroke's are oval; arched and padded in both breeds.

TAIL

Cardigan: long and brush-like. Pembroke: naturally short or traditionally docked.

GROUP

Working (KC, ANKC). Herding (AKC).

It is only since 1934 that the Kennel Club has recognized the two separate breeds of Corgi: the Cardigan and the Pembroke. Their origins are obscure, but some form of Corgi was known at the time of the Domesday Book. It was used as a cattle dog, trained to nip at the cows' heels to herd them, then dart quickly out of the way. The attraction for heels, either animal or human, is still very much part of the Corgi's make-up and should be firmly discouraged during early training.

The Pembroke Corgi is the more popular of the two breeds possibly because of its royal patronage, or because it has a slightly more outgoing nature. This is perhaps unfair on the Cardigan, which is more even tempered – the Pembroke can be snappy. It also has a powerful bark for such a small dog, and no inhibitions about using it. Both are affectionate and good with children, making loyal pets and effective guard dogs.

Like all low dogs, Corgis are vulnerable to chills. Rub them down carefully after they have been out in the cold or wet, paying particular attention to the stomach and chest.

Shetland Sheepdog

◄ *The semi-erect ears and enquiring look suggest the Shetland Sheepdog is ready for anything. This is probably true – it is a busy little dog and will want to be involved in all your activities.*

COAT

The outer coat is long, straight and wiry, while the white undercoat is soft, short and close to the body. There is a pronounced ruff and mane. For colours, see main text.

HEIGHT

Dogs: ideally 37 cm (14½ in); bitches: 35 cm (14 in). In Britain, no more than 2.5 cm (1 in) variation is permitted; in North America a height of up to 41 cm (16 in) is acceptable.

HEAD

In proportion to size of dog. A light, smooth wedge-shape, tapering to muzzle. Almond-shaped eyes. Small ears.

NECK

Muscular and well-arched.

BODY

Sturdy for the size of the dog. Deep chest, reaching as low as the elbows. A level back.

LEGS

Muscular. The hind legs are particularly well feathered. Oval, well-padded feet.

TAIL

Set low. Abundant feathering and slight upward curve.

GROUP

Working (KC, ANKC). Herding (AKC).

Despite its delicate appearance, dainty feet and luxurious coat, the Sheltie, as it is commonly known, is a tough little thing, full of character, determination and mischief. As its name suggests, it originates in the Shetland Islands in the north of Scotland – a place of which it has been said that there are nine months of winter and three months' bad weather. The Sheltie is therefore able to cope with the harshest of conditions. It was bred as a working dog and is perpetually on the go, capable of walks that would exhaust many a larger breed.

It looks very like a miniature Rough Collie, but in fact has been recognized as a breed in its own right since the early years of the 20th century. It may, indeed, have Icelandic dogs in its ancestry, brought over to the Shetlands in fishing boats.

The Sheltie comes in particularly attractive colours. It may be sable – black-tipped hairs on a background of gold, silver, tan or grey; tricolour – black, tan and white; or blue merle – silvery-blue interspersed with black. All colours may have white markings on the chest, mane, legs and tail tip.

Easy to train and very affectionate with its family, the Sheltie may be wary with strangers. It is intelligent but can be sensitive. It makes a useful guard dog, though the persistent high-pitched bark may not be to everyone's liking.

Hungarian Puli

A friendly companion, though tending to be a one-person dog, the Puli is also an excellent house dog, barking at any strange sound. Although it was bred as a sheepdog and is therefore used to open spaces, it can cope with being more confined as long as it is given plenty of exercise. ▶

COAT

Long and coarse outer coat, with a fluffy undercoat combining to make cords. Black, rusty black, white, grey or apricot.

HEIGHT

Dog: 40-44 cm (16-17½ in); bitch: 37-41 cm (14½-16 in). Up to 48 cm (19 in) in North America.

HEAD

Small and fine with bluntly rounded muzzle. Dark brown, lively eyes. Wide-set, V-shaped, drooping ears.

NECK

Of medium length and allowing head to be held high.

BODY

Deep ribcage; withers and short, broad loins are slightly higher than the back.

LEGS

Muscular with straight forelegs and well-bent stifles on hind legs.

TAIL

Medium length and curled tightly over the rump.

GROUP

Working (KC, ANKC). Herding (AKC).

Although its extraordinary hairstyle resembles Rastafarian dreadlocks, the Hungarian Puli's ancestry lies not in Ethiopia but in Tibet. It was brought to Hungary from Asia by the invading Magyars about a thousand years ago, and has worked there as a sheepdog ever since. The Puli is also a confident water retriever, hence its alternative name of Hungarian Water Dog.

The all-over cords are formed by the natural weaving together of the fine undercoat and long, coarse outer coat. The result is a weatherproof covering which enables the dog to work in the harsh conditions of its native land. Indeed, working Pulis in Hungary have thicker cords than those kept as pets in other countries.

Like most sheepdogs the Puli is lively and energetic, needing regular exercise. It tends to be a one-person dog and can be over-protective of that person; it is not keen on strangers or patient with small children. It therefore needs careful training and socialization, but can make a loyal and affectionate pet.

The Puli's cords need regular attention to stop them becoming matted and tangled. The cords should be carefully separated by hand, not combed, and the coat can then be lightly brushed.

Kelpie

The Kelpie is a hard-working dog with a steady temperament, but it needs firm discipline and early attention to socialization. Bred in Australia for 200 years, it has only recently become familiar in other parts of the world.

Not well known outside its native Australia, the Kelpie, or Barb, should nevertheless be familiar to anyone who has seen a newsreel about farming in this country – it is the breed that runs along the backs of the sheep it is herding. 'Kelpie' is the Gaelic word for water sprite, and was the pet name given to an early member of the breed and which survived to cover its offspring.

Reports of its origin agree that it is descended from British sheepdogs introduced into Australia by 18th-century settlers; they differ about whether or not it was crossed with the native dingoes to produce the modern breed. Certainly the fox-like shape of the head seems to owe more to the dingo than to the ancestor of the Border Collie.

Whatever the truth, the end result is a tough, solidly built but fleet-footed sheepdog, capable of working in the extreme conditions of the Australian climate and managing to go without water for surprising lengths of time. Like most sheepdogs, the Kelpie is intelligent, easy to train and extremely loyal to its owner.

Because it was bred to work in open spaces, it needs not only regular exercise, but also plenty of space. It will be miserable cooped up in an apartment or flat.

COAT

Thick, short and smooth. Colours range from black or black and chestnut through grey to red or tan.

HEIGHT

Dogs: 46-51 cm (18-20 in); bitches: 43-48 cm (17-19 in).

HEAD

Fox-like, with strong jaws. Pronounced stop. Brown, medium-sized, almond-shaped eyes. Erect, pointed ears.

NECK

Thick, longish, and very muscular.

BODY

Compact and solid, with a level back and not particularly deep chest.

LEGS

Muscular. Forelegs straight; hind legs with a pronounced bend at the stifle. Round feet.

TAIL

Coarse hair on the underside. Carried low but with a slight upward curve towards the tip.

GROUP

Working (KC, ANKC). Miscellaneous (AKC).

Samoyed

The Sammy is one of the most fun-loving of breeds – the alert, smiling expression means what it says! It will take all the exercise you can give it. Be warned, though: it will often express its enthusiasm loudly. ▶

COAT

Full, thick and straight, with a harsh, weather-resistant top coat and soft, short undercoat. Usually all white.

HEIGHT

46-56 cm (18-22 in). May be taller in North America.

HEAD

Strong, with a broad, flat skull and slightly tapering, medium-length muzzle. Almond-shaped, slanted brown eyes. Slightly rounded ears are carried erect.

NECK

Muscular and of medium length, arched so that the head is carried proudly.

BODY

Deep chest and ribs; broad, muscular back; strong loin and hindquarters.

LEGS

Medium length, the front legs being well-feathered. Long, well-feathered feet with widespread toes.

TAIL

Long and hairy; carried curled over the back.

GROUP

Working (KC, AKC). Utility (ANKC).

The Samoyedes were a people of northern Siberia, and this beautiful dog served them as sled puller, reindeer herder and guard dog; its luxuriant hair was also woven into warm outer garments.

Bred to survive some of the coldest temperatures on earth, the Samoyed, or Sammy, is extremely hardy and has tremendous powers of endurance. In this respect its career record speaks for itself as it was chosen to accompany Fridtjof Nansen on his journeys across the Arctic ice floes, as well as Roald Amundsen and Robert Falcon Scott on their expeditions to the South Pole. And it was probably Scott who introduced the dog to Australia in the course of his travels.

The Samoyed's beauty makes it an extremely popular show dog, and it is now bred largely for that purpose and as a companion. Naturally intelligent, loyal and responsive to training, it retains an independent streak and a boisterous love of life that may need to be restrained. Obedience classes should encourage it to toe the line. Its coat needs a lot of care and it will moult heavily in the spring.

A much smaller white Spitz dog, the Japanese Spitz, has recently been introduced into Britain and is growing in popularity. In North America, the Miniature and Toy American Eskimos are a good choice for those wanting a smaller Spitz dog.

Border Collie

◀ *Widely used as a working dog the world over, the Border Collie dominates sheepdog trials and exhibitions of obedience training.*

The Border Collie's name comes from the hilly country on either side of the border between England and Scotland where it was bred as a sheepdog. Although something like it has been around for several hundred years, the Kennel Club only recognized the breed in 1976. By that time it had been firmly established in Australia where it had been taken by settlers in the 18th century – and the British standard is partly based on that of the Australian National Kennel Council. The Border Collie still only has 'Miscellaneous' status in the United States and Canada.

Some admirers of the Border Collie expressed concern when it was officially recognized, lest emphasis on the 'standard' impaired the working qualities they cherished. But although the breed is becoming more popular as a pet and as a show dog, it is still first and foremost a worker: active, intelligent, eager and obedient. It can be sensitive and occasionally over-protective. There is no danger of losing your children if you have a Border Collie as a pet – it will herd anything that shows a tendency to wander! Although it will adapt to most lifestyles, it likes space and the outdoors, so is probably better suited to the country than to the town.

COAT

Can be moderately long or short. In either case, there is a dense, medium-textured outer coat and a softer undercoat. A range of colours is permitted, although black and white is the most common. White should not predominate.

HEIGHT

Dog: 53 cm (21 in); bitch slightly less.

HEAD

Fairly broad skull. Very distinct stop and tapering, shortish muzzle. Oval eyes, usually brown. Wide set, medium-sized ears carried erect or semi-erect.

NECK

Strong and of good length, broadening at the shoulders.

BODY

Longish, deep chested and athletic looking.

LEGS

Strong but not heavy, with oval, well-padded feet.

TAIL

Set low, longish with upward curve. Very bushy in long-haired animals.

GROUP

Working (KC, ANKC). Miscellaneous (AKC).

Bearded Collie

There is an intelligent and fun-loving face underneath all this hair. The Beardie is blessed with a happy nature and very little seems to upset it. ▶

COAT

In two layers, with a long, shaggy outer coat and soft, dense undercoat. A variety of colours, usually grey, black or reddish brown, with or without white markings.

HEIGHT

Dog: 53-56 cm (21-22 in); bitch: 51-53 cm (20-21 in).

HEAD

In proportion to the size of the dog. Broad, square skull. Moderate stop and strong, squarish muzzle. Prominent, hairy eyebrows. Drooping, medium-sized ears.

NECK

Of medium length, muscular and slightly arched.

BODY

Deep chested, with a long, strong ribcage. A level back.

LEGS

Muscular, with shaggy hair. Oval, well-padded feet, also covered with hair.

TAIL

Long and well-covered with hair. Slight curve near tip.

GROUP

Working (KC, ANKC). Herding (AKC).

The Beardie, as it is often called, is another of those dogs with an uncertain ancestry. Something like it has been known in Scotland for 2000 years, but today's Beardie is probably a descendant of those dogs crossed with Polish or Magyar immigrants in about the 15th century. In the early part of this century the breed was practically extinct and not deemed worthy of a pedigree, but in the 1940s a determined breeder sought out a male to mate with her Beardie bitch. All modern Beardies can claim descent from Jeannie and Bailie, the pair in question.

The Beardie bears a striking resemblance to the Old English Sheepdog, to which it is probably related. The long, shaggy coat is weather-resistant, well adapted to the cold and wet climate in which this breed has traditionally done most of its work. Beardies do not come into their full adult coat until they are two years old, so the puppies require extra brushing. For a mature dog, a daily brush is desirable and a careful going over once a week essential. As with all long-haired dogs, it is important to clean off mud after walks to prevent hair on the legs and stomach becoming tangled.

This is an active, friendly dog, requiring plenty of exercise but always ready to join in with games. It is good with children and makes an ideal family pet.

Rough Collie

◀ *Loyalty is the feature for which the Rough Collie is famous. It makes an excellent and protective family pet, devoted to its family but tending to be wary of strangers.*

The Rough or Scotch Collie is descended from Scottish sheepdogs and the breed owes its current status to Queen Victoria, who was captivated by the Collies working on the Balmoral estate. She brought several back to London with her, and the Polite World on both sides of the Atlantic adopted the breed which became very fashionable. The 1940s film *Lassie Come Home* and its sequels on both large and small screen have ensured that Rough Collies remain loved and respected for their loyalty and intelligence.

There are several breeds of Collie, but the Rough – the 'Lassie dog' – is the most popular. Prized nowadays for its thick, glossy coat, it is still a competent working dog given the chance. It needs a *lot* of grooming – it will look dreadful if its coat is neglected and will shed hair all over the house. The Smooth Coated Collie is considered a separate breed, but there are few differences apart from the length and texture of the coat.

Traces of the Rough Collie's ancestry may still show themselves when the dog is walking on hillsides or farmland, so keep your dog under control when there are sheep about.

COAT

Very dense, the outer coat being straight and stiff, while the undercoat is soft and furry. There is a pronounced ruff or mane. Colours may be sable and white, tricolour (black, tan and white) or blue merle, a clear silvery blue interspersed with black. All combinations have white markings.

HEIGHT

Dog: 56-61 cm (22-24 in); bitch: 51-56 cm (20-22 in). Both sexes are up to 5 cm (2 in) larger in North America.

HEAD

Almond-shaped eyes should have a sweet expression. Ears are semi-erect when dog is alert, but laid back in repose.

NECK

Strong and well-arched.

BODY

Long, deep chested.

LEGS

Muscular and well-feathered. Well-padded, oval feet.

TAIL

Long, well-feathered, usually carried low but with an upward curve near the tip.

GROUP

Working (KC, ANKC). Herding (AKC).

Boxer

The Boxer never loses its love of rough games – do not imagine, therefore, that your boisterous puppy is going to calm down when it reaches adulthood. Only really energetic people should consider acquiring a Boxer, but for the right owner it is a most rewarding dog. ▶

COAT

Short, smooth and glossy. May be fawn or brindle, with or without white markings.

HEIGHT

Dog: 57-63 cm (22½ -25 in); bitch: 53-59 cm (21-23 in).

HEAD

In proportion to the size of body, squarish with a pronounced stop. A broad, deep muzzle, well-padded upper lips, undershot jaw and upturned nose. Dark brown eyes are quite close together. Medium-sized ears are set wide apart.

NECK

Longish, elegantly arched.

BODY

Very deep chest and long ribcage. Short, broad back sloping slightly downwards.

LEGS

Long, straight and strong. Very muscular thighs. Front feet are small and cat-like; Hind feet are longer.

TAIL

Set high and carried upright; traditionally docked.

GROUP

Working (KC, AKC). Utility (ANKC).

The Boxer as we know it was developed in Germany not much more than 100 years ago. Its antecedents were Mastiff-like, used for bear-baiting in medieval Germany, but it was carefully crossed with other breeds, including the Bulldog, in an attempt to produce the ideal police dog. Breeders were looking for strength and stamina combined with agility, courage combined with controlled aggression, and considerable intelligence. All these qualities are highly developed in the Boxer, which is still frequently used for police work in Germany and as a guard dog in many countries the world over.

The Boxer's popularity outside its native land began when British and American soldiers took it with them as they returned home after the Second World War.

For all its power and potential fierceness, the Boxer makes a good pet. Naturally exuberant, it requires firm training from an early age and plenty of exercise throughout its life. It will become devoted to its owner and is fond of children as well as being an enthusiastic playmate.

CARE TIP

Dogs, like people, use body language to convey mood. In the wild, a dog may lie on its back exposing its belly to tell a dominant animal that it acknowledges its superiority. A domestic dog may adopt this submissive posture after being scolded.

Old English Sheepdog

The anarchic appearance of the Old English Sheepdog is deceptive. Originally a working dog, it is now kept mainly as a pet and it remains intelligent and reliable.

Related to the Bearded Collie, the Old English Sheepdog, or Bobtail, was first bred in the south west of England about 200 years ago, although it may have the Russian Owtscharka and the Briard in its ancestry. It was an all-purpose farmer's dog, used to round up the flocks and herds, guard them against attack and drive them to market. Even as a pet it retains the herding and guard dog instincts: it is protective of its owners and territory, and anxious if an individual strays too far from the group during a walk.

The Old English Sheepdog's style of walking can best be described as an ungainly amble, but in full gallop it is both athletic and elegant.

This is an affectionate breed, excellent with children and a good house dog. A mature dog can be quite docile and, despite its size, will live happily in a small home as long as it has lots of exercise. It also requires daily grooming, as one glance at its extraordinary coat can tell you.

CARE TIP

Old English Sheepdog puppies are boisterous but respond well to training. Teaching your dog to sit on command is a first step. Pressing the hindquarters downwards while repeating the command will help the dog understand what is required – and copious praise when it gets it right will reinforce the message.

COAT

Shaggy and coarse. The body and hindquarters may be grey, grizzle or blue, with a white head, chest and forelegs.

HEIGHT

(Minimum) dog: 61 cm (24 in) in Britain, 56 cm (22 in) in North America; bitch: 56 cm (22 in).

HEAD

Largish, square skull with well-defined stop. Short, strong, square muzzle. Wide set eyes, dark or blue. Small ears lie flat against the side of the head.

NECK

Longish, strong and arched.

BODY

Compact with deep brisket and narrow shoulders. The sturdy loins are higher than the withers.

LEGS

Forelegs straight, with elbows close in to the brisket. Thighs are long and muscular. Small, round feet with thick pads.

TAIL

May be naturally bobbed (traditionally docked if longer).

GROUP

Working (KC, ANKC). Herding (AKC).

Briard

Although it has been used for some gruelling tasks, the Briard has a playful disposition and enjoys boisterous games. ▶

COAT

Long, slightly wavy and very dry, with a fine, dense undercoat. Black, possibly with some white hairs, or fawn with dark shading.

HEIGHT

Dog: 62-68 cm (24-27 in); bitch: 56-64 cm (23-25½ in).

HEAD

Covered with long hair. Slightly rounded skull and square, strong muzzle. Quite large, dark-brown eyes. Shortish ears, covered with long hair.

NECK

Strong, muscular and well-arched.

BODY

Broad chest, firm and level back.

LEGS

Well-muscled. Large, strong, round feet. Legs and feet are well-covered with long hair.

TAIL

Long and covered with hair. Carried low, with a slight curve. May be docked in some countries.

GROUP

Working (KC, ANKC). Herding (AKC).

The Briard comes from the region of Brie in France, where it was known as early as the 12th century. It even appears in a medieval French legend as the winner of a duel against the man who had killed its master. It was bred as a dual-purpose sheepdog, both to herd animals and to guard them against attack. Legend also has it that it was introduced into North America in the 18th century, by either the Marquis de Lafayette or Thomas Jefferson, presumably to assist the Americans against the British in the War of Independence.

It is an energetic athlete, capable of running long distances; it is surprisingly agile and graceful for a dog with such a shaggy appearance.

Fearless and protective of its owner, but not aggressive, the Briard makes an excellent pet if you have the time to give it all the exercise it needs. The long coat, particularly the delightful fringe which hangs down over the eyes, needs plenty of grooming if it is not to become messy.

CARE TIP

Even if you don't want a working animal, you should teach your dog to obey simple commands. Instruct your dog to 'stay', then move away. If the dog moves, put it back in position and repeat the command firmly. Reward it when it obeys. Using a hand signal that a dog will associate with the verbal command is useful for situations when the dog cannot hear you.

German Shepherd Dog

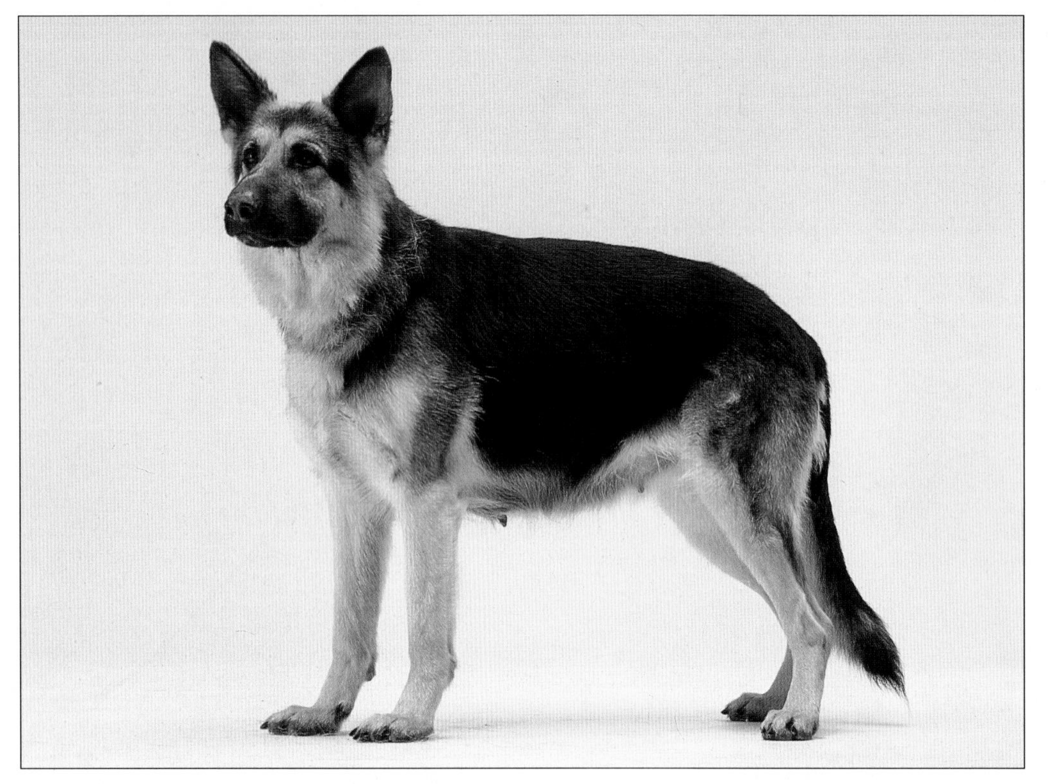

◀ *The German Shepherd can be taught to do almost anything, from guiding the blind to remaining calm in the face of gunfire. It will always carry out its tasks with enthusiasm.*

Now arguably the most popular breed in the world, the German Shepherd, or Alsatian, was developed in Germany at the end of the 19th century as a sheep dog, but its qualities as a guard and as a working dog with the police and the armed forces soon became apparent. British soldiers who had seen it in action during the First World War introduced the breed to Britain in the 1920s. It is also now widely recognized as an excellent guide dog for the blind.

The breed has its critics, but the tendency to aggression and overprotectiveness that some German Shepherds have shown is more to be blamed on bad handling and lack of socialization rather than on any innate fault in the dog. These are intelligent, potentially headstrong dogs. Like most intelligent breeds, Shepherds can become mischievous when bored. Properly trained, however, they are extraordinarily obedient – which means they can be taught to be gentle family pets as well as fearless guard dogs. When selecting puppies, look out for possible hip problems, to which the breed is prone, and be careful to select from sound stock to avoid problems of temperament.

CARE TIP

Muzzles come in various shapes and sizes and it is important that you choose one that is secure but not too tight. The Halti collar is half collar, half muzzle and is useful for restraining dogs which insist on pulling on the lead.

COAT

In two thick layers, the outer coat is flat and coarse and the undercoat particularly dense. Some males have a ruff. Colours range from black to mixtures of grey and yellow.

HEIGHT

Dogs: 62 cm (25 in); bitches: 57 cm (23 in). In North America 56-66 cm (22-26 in).

HEAD

Well-proportioned. Gradually tapering nose with no pronounced stop. Powerful, wedge-shaped muzzle. Strong jaws. Almond-shaped eyes, usually dark brown. The ears are set high and carried erect.

NECK

Long and strong.

BODY

Straight backed and deep chested.

LEGS

Straight, with back legs muscular and well-feathered. Rounded feet with hard wearing pads.

TAIL

Bushy, with a slight curve.

GROUP

Working (KC, ANKC). Herding (AKC).

Rottweiler

Although it is always wise to choose a puppy from a reputable breeder, this is particularly important with a Rottweiler. It is an immensely powerful dog,so you should be fully aware of the commitment to training and exercise that you are taking on. ▶

COAT

Medium length with coarse but glossy hair. Black with brown markings.

HEIGHT

Dog: 63-69 cm (25-27 in); bitch: 58-63 cm (23-25 in). May be slightly smaller in North America.

HEAD

Broad, with arched forehead, clearly defined stop and deep muzzle. Medium-sized, almond-shaped, dark brown eyes. Smallish ears, set high on the head but wide apart, hanging close to the head.

NECK

Longish, round, very muscular. Well-arched so that the head is carried proudly.

BODY

Broad, deep chest. Broad, strong back.

LEGS

Longish, muscular, with round, compact feet.

TAIL

Short and strong, carried horizontally. Has traditionally been docked.

GROUP

Working (KC, AKC). Utility (ANKC).

Rottweilers have had a bad press in recent years, but the fault lies more with overbreeding to cater for rapidly increasing popularity than with any inherent defect. The fact that the Rottweiler's undoubtedly rugged appearance has attracted a type of owner more interested in image than in the dog's good qualities has also not enhanced its reputation.

That said, the vast majority of Rottweilers are loyal and reliable dogs. They are wary of strangers and certainly prepared to defend their owners or territory if necessary, but they are affectionate with those they know. Although they tend to be one-person dogs, Rottweilers may also make good family pets.

The name originates from the German town of Rottweil, where the breed was developed in medieval times to help the local butchers herd cattle to market and protect them and their money on the way home. In more recent years, Rottweilers have been used as draught dogs, guard dogs and police dogs; they also played an important role for the German forces during the First World War.

CARE TIP

Two dogs sniffing each other's rear ends is a familiar sight whenever strange animals meet. They may decide to be friendly, or they may snarl and react aggressively. No serious harm is likely to come of this, as one dog will usually adopt a submissive posture, acknowledging the other's superior position.

Bernese Mountain Dog

◄ *The Bernese's docile expression and sturdy, four-square stance make it a picture of dependability. Certainly there are few breeds that make better family pets.*

There are four breeds of Swiss Mountain Dog, each native to small areas of the country. The Bernese is the only long-haired of the four, and certainly the most beautiful. It comes from the Swiss canton of Berne, where it was bred to pull carts for the local weavers and cheesemakers. It also worked as a guard and herd dog. Its complicated history goes back well over 2000 years, but the breed later went into decline and the modern Bernese is the result of a concerted effort to revive its strong points. It was only recognized outside Europe in the 1890s.

It is immensely loyal and, although slow to learn, is eager to please and completely reliable once it has grasped what is expected of it. It therefore needs gentle and patient training, but will reward this with obedience and devotion. It retains enough of its draught dog instincts to be willing to pull small carts at fairs and shows, which makes it a great favourite with children.

Being both large and long-haired, the Bernese needs plenty of exercise and grooming. It also has a hearty appetite. Anyone contemplating acquiring such a pet should be aware of the demands (and expense) of a big dog.

COAT

Long and silky, with a slight wave. Mostly black with striking tan and white markings.

HEIGHT

Dog: 64-70 cm (25-27½ in); bitch: 64-70 cm (23-26 in). In Canada dogs may be 6 cm (2½ in) smaller and bitches 2 cm (1 in) smaller.

HEAD

Strong with a flat skull and well-defined stop. Strong, straight muzzle and strong jaw. Dark brown, almond-shaped eyes. Triangular ears, lying flat in repose.

NECK

Of medium length, strong and muscular.

BODY

Compact. Broad chest, deep brisket reaching to the elbows. Level back and strong loins.

LEGS

Straight and well-muscled. Compact, round feet.

TAIL

Bushy, reaching to just below the hocks. Raised when alert, but not carried over the body.

GROUP

Working (KC, AKC). Utility (ANKC).

Dobermann

The Dobermann has a magnificent physique and an athletic gait – it is in fact a compact canine powerhouse. If you choose your puppy with care and train it properly, however, you will have an affectionate and obedient pet. ▶

COAT

Smooth, short and thick. May be black, blue, brown or fawn with rust red markings.

HEIGHT

Dog: 69 cm (27 in); bitch: 65 cm (25½ in). In North America, a range of 61-71 cm (24-28 in) is permitted.

HEAD

Long and flat with a slight stop. Long, wedge-shaped muzzle and strong jaw. Dark, almond-shaped eyes. Small, normally dropped ears.

NECK

Longish, allowing the head to be held nobly.

BODY

Square, with deep chest and ribcage and short, strong back, sloping downwards from shoulders to loins. Well tucked-up belly.

LEGS

Very straight, muscular forelegs. Powerful hind legs stretch well out behind the end of the body.

TAIL

Carried in line with the body; traditionally docked.

GROUP

Working (KC, AKC). Utility (ANKC).

The Dobermann Pinscher is one of the few breeds about whose origins it is possible to be absolutely definite. It was the creation of a German tax collector named Louis Dobermann who decided, in the 1860s, that he wanted a special dog to protect him in the course of his unpopular profession. Courage, strength, intelligence and an instinct to guard were the qualities he was looking for. *Pinscher* is the German word for terrier, and Dobermann's 'terrier' is believed to have contained elements of the Rottweiler, the Greyhound, the German Shepherd and the Weimar Pointer – as well as the German Pinscher and the Manchester Terrier.

The breed quickly became established and was used to support the German army during the First World War. British and American soldiers, impressed by the Dobermann's fortitude, took the dog home with them and it is now known throughout the world as an excellent guard or police dog and a loyal if strong-minded pet.

Early socialization and firm training are important, but it is naturally obedient and devoted to the people it knows. It has a hearty appetite and appreciates a daily run, but it is easy to groom and you won't have to worry about burglars.

CARE TIP

Short-haired dogs are susceptible to chills and few of them will be comfortable in outdoor kennels. Always dry your dog thoroughly when it comes in out of the rain and buy it a coat if the winter is particularly cold.

Newfoundland

◄ *The Newfoundland is the most docile and affectionate of dogs. It loves children, is devoted to its family and gets on well with other animals – a perfect companion. Like most big dogs, however, it requires space, exercise and plenty to eat.*

The Newfoundland may be as tall as a Great Dane and weigh as much as a Pyrenean Mountain Dog, but it can safely be left to look after children in the absence of an adult. It is the ultimate 'gentle giant'.

It originated in Europe and was taken to the eastern-most province of Canada by either the Vikings or by French settlers in the 17th century. On this weatherbeaten island the Newfoundland developed extraordinary skills in swimming and life saving, making it an indispensable companion to the local fishermen. Its thick coat enables it to withstand severe weather conditions; it is also endowed with remarkable strength, stamina and, like all natural rescue dogs, intelligence. On land, it can tow a small wagon, act as a guard dog and be one of the most affectionate and easy going of all pets.

In Britain it became very popular in the 19th century when Sir Edwin Landseer featured it in his painting 'A Distinguished Member of the Humane Society'. The dog he depicted was black and white, a colour combination that has since been described as 'Landseer' when it occurs in the Newfoundland.

COAT

In two thick layers, coarse and oily, forming a water-resistant covering. Black, brown or Landseer (see main text) are the accepted colours.

HEIGHT

Dog: 71 cm (28 in); bitch: 66 cm (26 in).

HEAD

Broad and massive, with short, square muzzle. Small ears lie close to the head; small, deep set, brown eyes.

NECK

Strong but not long.

BODY

Broad and deep-chested, with level back and strong loins.

LEGS

Straight and muscular; abundant feathering on forelegs, less on hind legs. Large webbed feet.

TAIL

Longish and hairy, but without feathering and only a slight curve towards the tip. Carried low in repose, straight out when excited.

GROUP

Working (KC, AKC). Utility (ANKC).

Pyrenean Mountain Dog

The Pyrenean Mountain Dog has a gentle expression that is particularly appealing in such a huge dog. There is a definite soft side to its nature, but it is also intelligent and hard working. ▶

COAT

In two layers, the outer longish, thick and coarse, the undercoat very dense and fine. All white, or mainly white with markings of grey, pale yellow or blaireau (brown/black/grey and white).

HEIGHT

(Minimum) dog: 70 cm (28 in); bitch: 65 cm (26 in).

HEAD

Strong, domed, with a slight furrow rather than an obvious stop. The powerful muzzle tapers slightly towards tip. Dark brown, almond-shaped eyes. Smallish, rounded ears.

NECK

Strong, thick, rather short.

BODY

Deep-chested with long, broad ribcage and broad, muscular, level back.

LEGS

Straight and muscular with strong thighs. Compact feet with strong nails.

TAIL

Long, well-covered with hair, with a slight kink to one side.

GROUP

Working (KC, AKC). Utility (ANKC).

The Pyrenean Mountain Dog, known in North America as the Great Pyrenees, stands over 60 cm (2 ft) at the shoulder and the males weigh 50 kg (110 lb). A dense coat over a massive body makes this one of the largest and most impressive looking of all breeds.

Descended from the Tibetan Mastiff, whose history goes back thousands of years, the Pyrenean Mountain Dog was confined to the Pyrenees for many centuries. It was bred as a sheepdog, to guard the flocks against attacks from bears or wolves.

Pyrenean Mountain Dogs were 'discovered' in the 17th century and taken to Paris. It soon became the fashion in France to have these magnificent white creatures, wearing the studded collar now usually seen on mastiffs, guarding a chateau.

The Pyrenean has an affectionate and tolerant nature, making it an excellent family pet. However, it is still by nature a guard dog and tends to react badly to advances from strangers. Although it can make do with surprisingly little exercise for such a large dog, it does like plenty of space.

CARE TIP

Give a dog tablets by offering them disguised as a treat – wrapped in soft cheese, for example. If the dog will not accept this, gently pull its jaws apart, put the tablet on its tongue, then hold the jaws shut. Stroking the throat will encourage the dog to swallow.

Mastiff

◄ *Plenty of space is the Mastiff's main requirement, although it only needs a moderate amount of exercise for its size. It also has a healthy appetite. Grooming, on the other hand, is very easy.*

This is one of the most ancient of British breeds – it may have arrived with Phoenician traders as long ago as the 6th century BC. The Romans took Mastiffs from Britain to Rome, where they appeared in the local show rings, fighting lions, bears and gladiators. In England in medieval times the breed was used in organized dog fights and bear baiting; it also played a part at the Battle of Agincourt.

The Mastiff's popularity declined from the 17th century onwards and it was practically unknown in Britain by the end of the Second World War. But by this time it was popular in the United States, and imported stock has led to a resurgence of the breed and a strengthening of its most admirable characteristics.

The Mastiff is an intelligent and friendly dog with a strong instinct to protect its owner – the aggression which used to be encouraged in the breed will now only surface if it perceives some sort of threat. But it is a powerful animal that needs careful early training and is happiest if kept occupied. The Mastiff's heavy body can put a strain on its long legs, making it prone to joint problems. Watch out for any stiffness or signs of pain; if so, consult your vet.

COAT

Short and close. Apricot, silvery fawn, dark fawn, or brindle. Black ears and muzzle, and black around the eyes.

HEIGHT

Dog: about 76 cm (30 in); bitch about 70 cm (27½ in). The Canadian standard calls for a much smaller dog, with a maximum height of 56 cm (22 in).

HEAD

Broad with a flat forehead and short, square muzzle. Slightly pendulous lips. Small, wide-set eyes, hazel or brown. Small, wide-set ears lie close to head.

NECK

Longish, very muscular and slightly arched.

BODY

Very wide with deep chest and muscular loins.

LEGS

Long, straight and large boned. Particularly muscular thighs. Large, round feet.

TAIL

High set, longish, broad at base but tapering to a point.

GROUP

Working (KC, AKC).
Utility (ANKC).

Great Dane

The Great Dane is a truly majestic animal, elegant and dashing. It is clean and easy to groom, an ideal house dog if you don't mind it sleeping on the sofa or taking up a great deal of space in front of the fire. ▶

COAT

Short and sleek in a range of colours: brindle, black, fawn, blue or harlequin (white with black or blue patches).

HEIGHT

(Minimum) dog: 76 cm (30 in); bitch: 71 cm (28 in).

HEAD

Almost rectangular, with broad, longish muzzle and comparatively narrow skull. Strong jaw. Eyes are deep set and usually dark. Triangular ears.

NECK

Long and well-arched, so that the head is held high.

BODY

Deep brisket and well drawn-up belly giving an elegant curve to the underside of the body. Powerful shoulders and hindquarters. Strong back. Slightly arched loins.

LEGS

Very long and muscular. Cat-like feet.

TAIL

Longish, tapering from a broad base to a point.

GROUP

Working (KC, AKC). Non-sporting (ANKC).

The Great Dane has been a recognized show breed on both sides of the Atlantic since the latter half of the 19th century, but its origins probably date back to Roman times. There is no evidence that it came from Denmark; in fact, its alternative name, German Mastiff, which is a literal translation of the common German name, is a more accurate reflection of its pedigree. It has long been a popular breed in Germany, where it was a favourite of Chancellor Bismarck over 100 years ago.

Once a fierce creature much used as a guard and hunting dog, the Great Dane has been bred to become more docile and is now a reliable pet. For this, credit must go to North American breeders, who worked to control the dog's aggression. The Great Dane is still far from being very gentle, but careful selection has given it more control over its instincts. It is good with children and easy going with other animals, making it a devoted and affectionate family dog. Adult Great Danes require a lot of exercise and feeding, so a prospective owner should be prepared to make the necessary commitment in both time and money.

CARE TIP

Especially in towns and cities, responsible dog owners do not leave their pets' messes for someone else to tread on or clear up. 'Pooper scoopers' are readily available and cheap: take one with you on walks and put your dog's mess in the nearest bin.

Chihuahua

◀ *The Chihuahua is fearless, protective of whatever it considers its own – people, territory or toys – and very affectionate with people it knows. It is an ideal pet for an elderly person, or for anyone living in a flat or apartment.*

Although Chihuahua is a town in Mexico and the ancestors of the modern breed came to the United States from 'south of the border' about 100 years ago, experts differ about whether or not the dog is a native of Latin America. Some say it was known there in Aztec times, others that it was introduced by the Spanish conquistadors in the 16th century having originated in Egypt.

The Chihuahua quickly earned fame and popularity as the smallest dog in the world. Originally exclusively smooth coated, it was crossed with other toy breeds to produce the long-haired variety which is gaining in popularity.

Chihuahuas can be delicate, so you should be sure to select your puppy from sound stock. As a breed they are fussy eaters, prone to stomach complaints. They prefer two or three small meals a day to one large one. They also hate the cold.

The Chihuahua is an intelligent, cheerful dog requiring little exercise and, in the case of the smooth-haired variety, little grooming. Its one drawback is that it is not good with children.

COAT

Smooth, soft and shiny, or long, soft and wavy with plenty of feathering. May be any colour or mixture of colours.

HEIGHT

About 15-22 cm (6-9 in). The standard specifies a weight: ideally 0.9-1.8 kg (2-4 lb). Less than 0.5 kg (1 lb) is acceptable in North America.

HEAD

Rounded skull, distinct stop, lean face and shortish, slightly tapering muzzle. Large, round eyes. Large, outward-pointing ears, well-feathered in the long-haired variety.

NECK

Of medium length and slightly arched.

BODY

Longish for the size of the dog, with a deep brisket, level back and strong hindquarters.

LEGS

Straight, with small, dainty feet.

TAIL

Of moderate length, carried high over back. Well-feathered in long-haired variety.

GROUP

Toy.

Pekingese

Although the Pekingese prefers its comforts to the rigours of a long walk, underneath that wilful exterior is a playful creature with a sense of mischief. ▶

COAT

Long, straight and flowing; in two layers, with coarse top coat and thick undercoat. Albino and liver are the only unacceptable colours.

HEIGHT

About 15-23 cm (6-9 in), with a maximum weight of 5 kg (11 lb) for dogs and 5.5 kg (12 lb) for bitches. Just over 6 kg (14 lb) is permitted in North America.

HEAD

Large and broad, with a flat skull, pronounced stop and short, wide, wrinkled muzzle. Large, round, dark eyes. Ears heart-shaped and feathered

NECK

Short and solid.

BODY

Short and sturdy with a broad chest, noticeable waist and level back.

LEGS

Short and solid, with the hind legs slightly lighter than the forelegs. Large, flat feet.

TAIL

Feathered. Carried over back with slight curve to one side.

GROUP

Toy.

One of the most ancient of all breeds, the Pekingese was kept in luxury in China for many centuries. It resembles the ancient Foo Dog which was once believed to ward off evil spirits.

As late as the 19th century the breed held an exalted position in Peking; when the British sacked the city in 1860, legend has it that the imperial family ordered all the dogs to be slain, to preserve them from the 'foreign devils'. A handful survived and were brought to England, where one was presented to Queen Victoria.

It is little wonder that the Pekingese has an aristocratic air. Not very reliable with children, it is independent and can be rather aloof, but is capable of great affection and expects plenty of attention. Modern Pekes are prone to heart and breathing problems, so should never be over-exercised in hot weather.

The Pekingese needs to be brushed and combed frequently to maintain its regal splendour.

CARE TIP

A Peke's eyes tend to weep, so they should be cleaned regularly with a soft pad of cotton wool, moistened in tepid water or a human eyewash. Consult your vet if the weeping seems excessive or if it is causing the dog distress. The Pomeranian *(see page 94)* *is another breed prone to this complaint.*

Griffon Bruxellois

◀ *Like many small dogs, the Griffon will make do with short walks, but it can keep up with you on longer treks and enjoy a good run.*

Three distinct breeds of this little Belgian terrier – the Brussels Griffon, the Belgian Griffon and the Petit Brabançon – are recognized in Europe. The British and American Kennel Clubs combine all three which they call the Griffon Bruxellois or the Brussels Griffon, allowing variations in texture and colour of coat which correspond to the differences between the European breeds. Smooth-coated and rough-coated Griffons do occasionally appear in the same litter.

Closely related to the Affenpinscher (see page 90) and with a similar 'cheeky monkey' expression, the Griffon has been popular in Belgium for centuries. It was bred as a street and stable dog, to control vermin, and it remains a tough and energetic little animal. It makes an affectionate and loyal pet with a happy and playful nature.

The rough-coated varieties need stripping, ideally by a professional, once or twice a year. Rubbing over with a hound glove with bristles or rubber dimples will keep the smooth-coated Petit Brabançon in good condition.

CARE TIP

If you are taking a small dog any distance in the car, it may be happier in a portable kennel. Choose a container large enough for your dog to stretch out in comfort, and make sure it travels with a favourite toy or blanket. Remember to stop regularly to give it water and allow it to relieve itself.

COAT

Either harsh and wiry or smooth and close-fitting. May be red, black or black and tan.

HEIGHT

About 20 cm (8 in), but the standard specifies a weight: ideally 2.7-4.5 kg (6-10 lb). In North America 5.5 kg (12 lb) is acceptable.

HEAD

Large for the size of the dog. Broad, rounded skull with deep stop. Very short, broad, turned-up muzzle. The rough-haired varieties have a full beard and moustache. Large, round, dark eyes. Small, wide set, semi-erect ears.

NECK

Of medium length and slightly arched.

BODY

Short but stocky; deep, broad chest, level back; strong loins.

LEGS

Forelegs straight, hind legs with well-bent stifles. Rough-haired varieties well-feathered.

TAIL

Carried erect but normally docked.

GROUP

Toy.

Papillon

The Papillon's fly-away ears and alert, eager expression add greatly to its appeal. It should be groomed every day to keep its long, silky coat in good condition. ▶

COAT

Long, silky and flowing. White combined with any colour except liver; or tricolour: white, black and tan.

HEIGHT

20-28 cm (8-11 in).

HEAD

Slightly rounded skull with clear stop. Fine, pointed muzzle. Medium-sized, round, dark eyes. Large, wide set ears with round tips and abundant feathering; may be erect or drop.

NECK

Of medium length.

BODY

Longish with deep chest, level back, slightly tucked-up belly and strong loins for the size of the dog.

LEGS

Straight, slender and abundantly feathered; hind legs with well-bent stifle. Delicate, hare-like feet with long tufts of hair between the toes.

TAIL

Long and plume-like, carried high over the back.

GROUP

Toy.

Papillon is French for butterfly, and one glance at this dog will show how it got its name – the disproportionately large ears are set wide apart, giving the head a distinct butterfly appearance.

The Papillon has been known in Europe for at least 500 years. Louis XV's powerful mistress Madame de Pompadour was a famous patron of the breed; another was Marie Antoinette who, according to one romantic tale, carried her Papillon with her to the guillotine. Legend does not record what happened to the dog.

In Europe a breed called the Phalene, which has drop ears, is considered separate from the Papillon; elsewhere the two breeds are treated as one, with both drop (or 'moth') and prick ears accepted.

Intelligent, lively and affectionate with its owner, the Papillon does, however, tend to be possessive and often objects to visitors. It may also be jealous of new babies.

Perhaps surprisingly, this delicate-looking dog has a history of success in obedience classes. Even if you don't want to go in for obedience training at a competitive level, the Papillon is very easy to train.

Yorkshire Terrier

◀ *Do not be misled by the fact that the Yorkie features on chocolate boxes and sentimental greetings cards. This is a tough little dog with a lot of character.*

Bred originally to control rats in the Yorkshire coal mines, the Yorkshire Terrier, or Yorkie, has elements of various Scottish terriers – the old Black and Tan Terrier and the Maltese are in its ancestry. It was intended to be a spirited companion for miners who would have found it difficult to keep a large dog.

From the most plebeian of beginnings it became, by the end of the 19th century, an aristocratic lap dog. Despite almost 100 years of pampering, it remains a hardy creature with a terrier's instincts: it is a keen hunter, an excellent guard dog and an enthusiastic walker. Its coat requires a lot of grooming, but it is otherwise easy enough to care for.

Utterly fearless, the tiny Yorkie is not intimidated by mere size. Although it is not aggressive, it will easily hold its own in an encounter with a much larger dog. It is friendly, outgoing, bouncy and affectionate – altogether a delightful companion.

CARE TIP

A double-sided brush is a useful tool for grooming a long-haired dog. The longer, wider spaced bristles reach through the coat to the dog's skin and allow for thorough brushing to remove mats. The shorter, denser bristles are ideal for finishing off or for a quick tidy up between serious grooming sessions.

COAT

Long, straight and silky. Dark steel blue with tan head and chest.

HEIGHT

Up to about 23 cm (9 in), but the standard specifies a maximum weight of 3 kg (7 lb).

HEAD

Small and flat, with shortish muzzle. The skull is covered with long hair, often forming a top knot. Medium-sized dark eyes. Small, V-shaped, well-feathered ears, carried erect.

NECK

Of moderate length and strength.

BODY

Compact with level back.

LEGS

Short, straight and well-covered with hair. Round feet.

TAIL

Darker in colour than the rest of the body, well-feathered and carried slightly above back level. Has traditionally been docked.

GROUP

Toy.

Bichon Frisé

The Bichon is a friendly, extrovert dog with a generally happy nature and an appealing bounce to its walk. It very much enjoys being part of a family. ▶

COAT

Soft, longish and curly. White coat with dark skin.

HEIGHT

23-28 cm (9-11 in), slightly taller in North America.

HEAD

In proportion to the size of the dog. Slightly rounded skull with height exaggerated by profuse hair. Moderate stop and shortish, medium-sized muzzle with large, round nose. Largish, round, dark eyes. Low-set ears hang close to the head and are well-covered with hair.

NECK

Longish, arched so that the head is carried proudly.

BODY

Sturdy, with deep brisket and broad, slightly arched loins.

LEGS

Straight and well-covered with hair. Hind legs have broad thighs and well-bent stifles. Tight, round feet.

TAIL

Neither high nor low set and curved elegantly over back.

GROUP

Toy (KC). Non-sporting (AKC).

The Bichon, as its alternative names, Bichon Tenerife or Tenerife Dog, suggest, probably originated in the Canary Islands, but it was brought to Malta and to countries around the Mediterranean as early as the 14th century. It was a favourite of aristocrats in France and Spain, then went out of fashion around 1800 and later became popular as a circus performer and street entertainer.

The breed seems to have dwindled until the time of the First World War, when British soldiers serving in France were struck by it and were eager to take it home. This apparently caused the French to reassess the worth of their home-grown product, and the breed was recognized in France in the 1930s. But it took another 50 years for it to attain breed status in Britain and the United States.

The Bichon should be brushed thoroughly every day, bathed about once a month, and trimmed whenever necessary to give its coat the appealing 'powder puff' effect. The breeder from whom you buy your puppy can advise you on exactly what to do, but you should be aware that keeping a Bichon smart is a time-consuming activity.

Affenpinscher

◀ *The Affenpinscher's shaggy coat does not need to be trimmed, although it should be brushed regularly to keep it shiny and healthy. The air of studied negligence is part of the breed's charm.*

Affen is the German for monkey, and this quaint little dog was once known in English as the Monkey Dog because of its mock serious monkey-like air. It is German in origin and a dog resembling the Affenpinscher appeared in Flemish and German paintings as early as the 15th century, making this one of the oldest of the toy breeds. Although it has been established in North America for over 50 years, it was only recognized in Britain in the 1980s.

The modern Affenpinscher is a true terrier despite its size – excellent at controlling vermin and happy chasing rabbits in the open when the opportunity arises. It is an alert, self-confident individual with a stubborn streak and a fearsome temper when it needs to defend itself.

It has the typical terrier inquisitiveness, so it will be into everything given the chance but it is eager to please and naturally obedient. It is devoted to its family and makes an affectionate pet, suitable for town or country. It is a robust dog, despite its size. Although it does not need much exercise, it will enjoy whatever you can give it and will appreciate the occasional really good run.

COAT

Harsh and rough; shaggy on the head, neck and shoulders, shorter on the rest of body and legs. Black, but may have grey shading.

HEIGHT

24-28 cm (9½-11 in). Maximum 25 cm (10 in) in North America.

HEAD

Small, with domed forehead, distinct stop and short, blunt muzzle. Medium-sized, dark, round eyes. Small, high set ears are usually carried erect.

NECK

Short and straight.

BODY

Short but sturdy.

LEGS

Forelegs straight. Hind legs well set under the body. Compact, round feet.

TAIL

Shortish, set high on the body and carried erect or gently curling over the back. May be docked in the United States and Canada.

GROUP

Toy.

Pug

The Pug's wrinkled face can give it a wistful appearance, but its expression easily becomes animated, even mischievous. Very much part of the family, the Pug will graciously accept all the attention you care to give it – and soon let you know if this is not enough. ▶

COAT

Short, smooth and glossy. May be silver, apricot or fawn with a black muzzle, ears and markings on the head, or all black.

HEIGHT

About 25-28 cm (10-11 in), and the standard specifies a weight: 6-8 kg (14-18 lb).

HEAD

Large for the size of the dog, round with wrinkled forehead and cheeks. Short, square muzzle. Large, round, dark eyes. Small, velvety ears folded forwards.

NECK

Strong and thick, slightly arched so that the head is carried proudly.

BODY

Short, broad and sturdy with level topline.

LEGS

Of medium length and very strong. Feet neither hare-like nor cat-like.

TAIL

Set on high and curled tightly over back.

GROUP

Toy.

This sturdy little dog has a long and varied history. Known in China for many centuries, it may be related to the Pekingese, but it also bears a strong resemblance to a miniature Mastiff. It was brought to Holland in the 16th century by traders with the Dutch East India Company, and quickly became a favourite of the ruling House of Orange.

William of Orange, who became William III of England in 1688, brought the Pug to Britain, where it remained a royal favourite. During the civil unrest in Holland 100 years later the Pug became the royalist symbol – and its status also led the rebels to adopt a dog, the less aristocratic Keeshond.

The name 'Pug' probably derives from 'puck', the impish spirit of Shakespeare's *A Midsummer Night's Dream*. There is nothing fairylike about the Pug's demeanour, but in Elizabethan times the word had a broader use as a general term of endearment. The Pug is also known as Mopse or Carlin.

The Pug is now a popular pet, affectionate, intelligent, easy to care for, good-natured and excellent with children. Although it enjoys exercise, it has a tendency to respiratory problems and should not be allowed to rush about too much or to become overheated.

Maltese

◀ *Although it has always been bred as a pet and looks as if it should stay indoors and keep its pretty coat clean, the Maltese loves to play. It is a healthy and active dog which enjoys the company of children.*

The Maltese is almost certainly the oldest of the European toy breeds. The Phoenicians, who were great seafaring traders, colonized Malta in about 1000 BC and were probably responsible for carrying the local dog far and wide on their travels. Certainly something like the Maltese was known in Egypt at about that time. However, a different version of the dog's history says that it originated not in Malta but in Sicily and that its name comes from the Sicilian town of Melita.

It has been suggested that the Maltese was brought to Britain when the Romans invaded in 55 BC, but it is more likely that it came back from Europe or the Middle East with returning Crusaders. Whatever the truth of this is, it was certainly established as a popular lap dog by the time of Elizabeth I.

Anyone who is not prepared to make a commitment to the task of thorough daily grooming should not contemplate acquiring a Maltese. The coat needs very gentle brushing and combing to preserve the silky texture. But your dog will reward you with great devotion – this is both an intelligent and a sweet-natured breed.

COAT

Longish, straight and silky. White, with or without lemon markings.

HEIGHT

Maximum 25 cm (10 in). In North America a maximum weight of just over 3 kg (7 lb) is specified, with a smaller dog preferred.

HEAD

Well-balanced, with definite stop, well filled-out face and broad muzzle. The long hair forms a fringe or top-knot. Dark brown, oval eyes are set quite close together. Long pendulous ears are well-covered with hairs.

NECK

Of medium length.

BODY

Short and sturdy, but well-proportioned with a level back.

LEGS

Short, with round feet.

TAIL

Well-feathered and carried in a curl over back.

GROUP

Toy.

Cavalier King Charles

One of the most lovable and loving of breeds, the Cavalier combines a fearless temperament with great gentleness and complete devotion to its owner.

COAT

Long and silky, with abundant feathering. May be black and tan, ruby, Blenheim (chestnut and white) or tricolour (black and white with tan markings).

HEIGHT

About 28 cm (11 in).

HEAD

Flat skull, shallow stop, full face and short, but not squashed, muzzle. Large, round, dark eyes set wide apart. Long, pendulous, well-feathered ears set high on the skull.

NECK

Of medium length and slightly arched.

BODY

Well-proportioned, with well-rounded ribs.

LEGS

Forelegs straight, hind legs with well-bent stifles. Compact feet, well-padded and feathered.

TAIL

Of a good length and abundantly feathered, carried jauntily.

GROUP

Toy (KC, CKC, ANKC). Miscellaneous (AKC).

King Charles II developed the King Charles Spaniel in the 17th century, though the toy spaniel was not a new concept and its ancestors may have originated in China centuries earlier. The breed became popular throughout Europe and was painted by Rubens, Rembrandt and Gainsborough. In those days it resembled the modern Cavalier, but as time went by it became smaller and more snub-nosed. The Cavalier is the result of a 20th century attempt to resurrect the qualities of the original breed, and was recognized in Britain in 1945.

The Cavalier likes its creature comforts – it is no coincidence that so many firedogs are moulded in the form of King Charles Spaniels, and the Cavalier is often to be seen sitting or lying as close to the fire as it can get. But this is also a sporting breed, fond of outdoor activities and long walks off the lead.

An affectionate companion for young and old, the Cavalier is always cheerful and eager to please. It is easy to look after; although the long coat needs frequent, thorough brushing, this is not a breed that needs expert trimming. The long ears should be checked regularly for infection and any matted hair removed.

CARE TIP

Many long-haired breeds have hairs between their pads: these should be trimmed regularly to avoid matting which would be uncomfortable. The best tool for this job is a pair of blunt-ended scissors.

Pomeranian

Regular brushing is essential to keep the Pomeranian looking like a bouncy ball of fluff. The hair should stand away from the body in a continuous mane that extends from the head to the hindquarters.

The Pomeranian is the smallest of the German Spitz dogs and is still registered as the Toy Spitz in Europe. It was well known throughout Europe in the 18th and 19th centuries, when it was a much larger dog than it is today. Queen Victoria brought a Pomeranian back to Britain with her after a visit to Germany in 1888. Her preference was for smaller dogs and this rapidly became the norm, with the smaller Pom enjoying huge success as a fashionable lap dog. It endured a slight fall from favour when the Pekingese emerged from China and became all the rage, but over the years the Pom has held its own and it remains popular today.

Like many of the toy breeds, it is a frequently pampered pet that is surprisingly alert and intelligent. Its quick, dainty gait makes it look as though it picks its way between muddy puddles, but it enjoys long walks. It has an independent nature and can amuse itself quite happily, but will respond to attention and make an affectionate and obedient pet. A tendency to yap should be discouraged by early training.

CARE TIP

Tiny dogs often have problems with their teeth, so check them regularly. An adequate supply of crunchy food or a rawhide bone to chew helps keep tartar at bay, but if small amounts appear regularly, brush your dog's teeth with a toothbrush or a moistened cotton bud. Canine toothpastes are available but are not essential to use. Large quantities of tartar should be removed by the vet.

COAT

In two layers, with a long, straight, harsh top coat and soft, fluffy undercoat. Any colour except black or white.

HEIGHT

About 30 cm (12 in). In North America a maximum height of 28 cm (11 in) is specified.

HEAD

Fox-like, with a comparatively large skull and short, fine muzzle. The skull is well-covered with mane-like hair. Medium-sized, dark, oval eyes. Small, erect ears.

NECK

Shortish.

BODY

Compact and well-rounded, with a deep chest and short back.

LEGS

Length in proportion to the size of the dog, fine-boned and well-feathered. Forelegs straight, hind legs with moderately bent stifles.

TAIL

Well-covered with hair, set on high and carried flat over the back.

GROUP

Toy.

Italian Greyhound

The Italian Greyhound's graceful appearance shows why it has been a favourite companion for so many centuries. It is affectionate and easy to train, but does not like being scolded. ▶

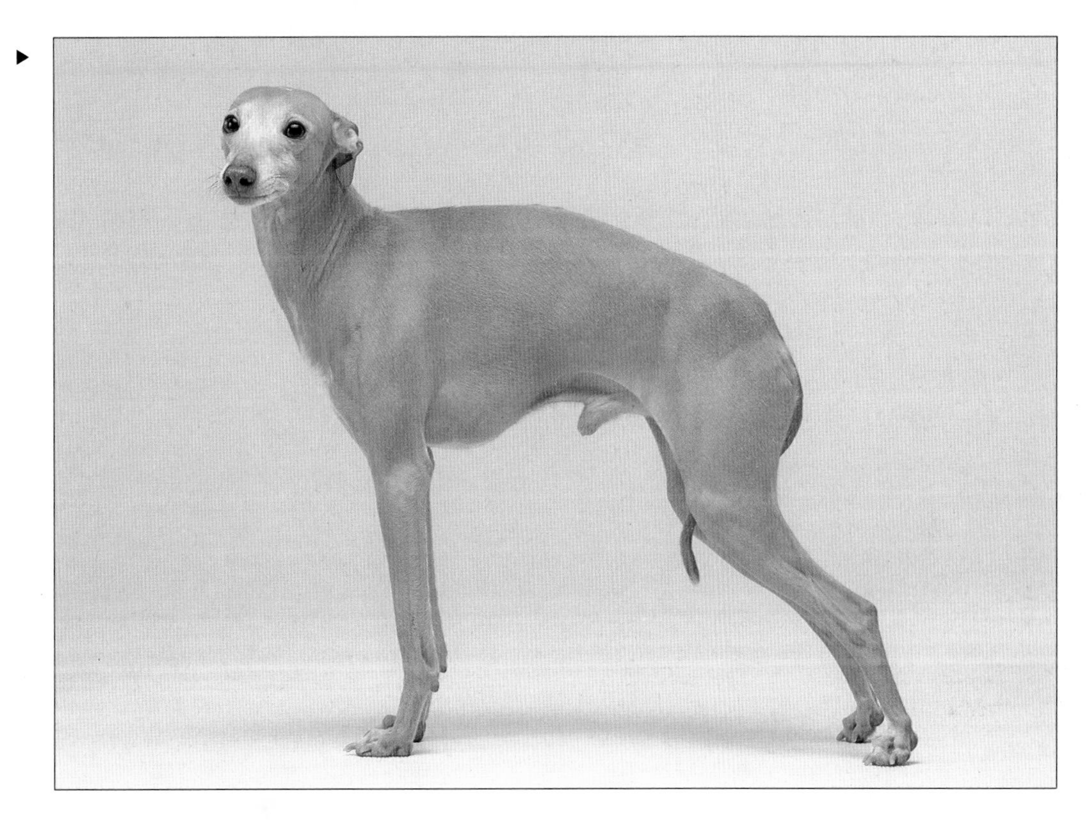

COAT

Short, fine and shiny. May be any colour except black and tan, blue and tan or brindle.

HEIGHT

About 32-38 cm (13-15 in), and the standard specifies a weight of 2.5-4.5 kg (6-10 lb). In North America there are two categories: over and under about 3.5 kg (8 lb).

HEAD

Flat skull and long, narrow muzzle. Largish, bright eyes. Soft, rose-shaped ears set well back on the head.

NECK

Long and elegant.

BODY

Slim, with deep chest, slightly arched loin and belly well tucked-up.

LEGS

Long for the size of the dog. Forelegs straight; long, muscular thighs and well-bent stifles. Hare-like feet.

TAIL

Long and fine, set low on the body and carried low.

GROUP

Toy.

The Greyhound is an ancient breed and a petite version was known in Egypt at the time of the Pharaohs. The Italian Greyhound as we know it was developed during the time of the Roman Empire, which makes it about 2000 years old. It was popular throughout Europe from the Middle Ages onwards, with royal patrons including Mary Queen of Scots and Frederick the Great of Prussia. Like so many toy breeds, it became particularly fashionable in England during the 19th century because Queen Victoria had one as a pet.

By the end of the 19th century, the mania for ever smaller dogs had done a great deal of damage to the Italian Greyhound in Europe, and the two world wars did further damage to its numbers. Larger and stronger specimens existed in the United States and Canada, but rebuilding the characteristics of the breed took a great deal of time and effort. The Italian Greyhound remains a sensitive dog and is often seen trembling with emotion, in need of a reassuring pat.

Like its larger cousin, the Italian Greyhound is an athlete, capable of great bursts of speed; it needs good, regular runs. It feels the cold, though, so do not keep it in an outdoor kennel, and make sure that it is properly dried when it comes in from a rainy walk. A winter coat may be a good investment.

PHOTOGRAPHIC ACKNOWLEDGEMENTS

All photographs by Ray Moller, except those listed below.

The publishers would like to thank the agency and photographers who supplied us with the photographs reproduced on the following pages:

Cogis, Versailles/Isabelle Français 63; Marc Henrie 35, 54

The publishers would also like to thank Sue Boorman, Animal House and Handsome Hounds who arranged for the dogs to be photographed, and to all the the dog owners who so kindly cooperated.

Thanks are also due to Ann Taggart, MRCVS, for her expert advice regarding the text.